Obstacle
Course
on
Capitol Hill

Books by Robert Bendiner

White House Fever

Obstacle Course on Capitol Hill

Obstacle Course on Capitol Hill

By ROBERT BENDINER

McGraw-Hill Book Company

TORONTO
LONDON
NEW YORK

Preface

The Congress of the United States is altogether too necessary and admirable an institution to have its functioning and fate left exclusively to congressmen. To be sure, they know its processes best, and as American citizens they are entitled to as much say on the subject as the rest of us. But hardly more. For, being closest to it, they are the most easily blinded by its institutional lights, the most inhibited by personal loyalties from promoting changes that may be sorely needed. Quite possibly Congress will in time join the Athenian Assembly, the Roman Senate, and Tammany Hall among the civic monuments of history, but hopefully that time is far off. Before the cataclysm that brings it about, few needs can be more pressing than the periodic renewal of our national legislature, its recurrent adjustment to the times, its rearrangement now and again, the better to serve its purpose as the most effective possible instrument of popular government.

To examine the institution for weaknesses in this spirit is surely no more to disparage it than it is disparaging for a doctor to check from time to time on the organic workings of a patient. Though the reader is aware that the patient gener-

5

ally pays his doctor for this service while my attentions to
Congress are entirely gratuitous, possibly even unwanted, I
hope he will allow the comparison, understanding that such
criticisms as he finds in this book are made wholly out of
concern for the health of Congress at a time when it seems
more than normally in need of freshening. Emphatically they
are not to be regarded as part of a growing and dangerous
worship of executive power at the expense of the legislative,
a worship strangely common now among liberals, who should
be the last to put their trust in princes. Neither are such
criticisms intended to give aid and comfort to those who would
strip power from the national lawmakers in order to bestow
it upon state legislatures, which by contrast cause the Congress of the United States to shine with a statesmanship un-
known since the Age of Pericles.

In this sympathetic endeavor I find myself in a wide-ranging
company, for the improvement of Congress is happily an issue
that crosses both party and ideological lines. Name Democrats
like Clark, Humphrey, Douglas, Reuss, Bolling and Proxmire
as leaders in the current movement for change, and you are
obliged to add those of Republican leaders Case, Cooper,
Javits, Curtis, and Lindsay. Recall Democratic Senator Mon-
roney's part in the last significant reorganization, in 1946, and
you must also recall that of his Republican partner, the late
Senator La Follette. It was, in fact, the late Senator Kenneth
Wherry, a Republican of the deepest conservative dye and a
man given to practically no philosophical reflection whatever,
who said, "The machinery of Congress is so appallingly inadequate for modern times that free, representative government
is endangered."

To examine this machinery I have chosen an intertwining
pattern of the general and the particular. I propose, that is, to
consider alternately a major aspect of Congress—the committee
system, proceedings on the floor, the power of the Rules Com-

mittee—and then, in each case, to pursue the effect of that institutional aspect on a single major issue.

For purposes of illustration I needed an issue with a long, varied, and frustrating life history, and I had no trouble therefore in choosing Federal aid to the elementary and secondary schools of the country. To present as clearly and simply as possible a matter that circumstances have made muddy and complex, I have avoided dealing with aid to the colleges, a book in its own right, and, except tangentially, with those narrow special-purpose programs that Congress has embarked on from time to time in the field of education. For the most part I have confined myself to the proposal for general-purpose, all-around Federal aid to the primary and secondary schools, a proposition that, sporadically for over a century and almost biannually since World War II, has been beaten down in every way known to parliamentary man. Nearly a century of Congressional debate, volume after volume of testimony, compromise after compromise, have yet to produce such legislation, although bills to this end have been passed by House or Senate no fewer than ten times since the Civil War.

Given my purpose, I am not basically concerned in this book with the merits of the Federal aid issue as such. I do not pretend that I am indifferent to it or refrain from showing my personal sympathy for such legislation, but I wish to make it clear that my views in this matter are irrelevant to the major theme of the book. What I am chiefly concerned with here are the workings, or nonworkings, of Congress, the school bills being merely exemplary. Nevertheless, for those who are interested in the issue itself, I hope the book will serve incidentally as at least a sketchy narrative of its life and hard times in Washington.

As a final word on the limits of my purpose, I herewith renounce any pretense that what follows is a full and com-

prehensive study of the ways of Congress. Scores of parliamentary practices, dozens of Congressional maneuvers, will
be totally ignored in the effort to present a simple account of
the difficulty of getting a major issue resolved by Congress;
to give a sense of the overwhelming negativism that has come
dangerously close to becoming that body's chief characteristic.
For the general reader this seems to me more important than
an attempt to convey in all their minute and often dull detail
the technical mysteries of House and Senate procedure. Few
members of Congress themselves ever attempt to master this
body of arcana, preferring to leave such matters to the official
parliamentarians of the two chambers, and I suspect that the
reader will want to follow their example.

   Probably no book of this sort is written without real help
from others, certainly no book of mine. Besides acknowledging
the assistance I have had from general works on the ways of
Congress, listed elsewhere in this volume, I am happy to
record more particular debts, as follows: To Professor Richard
F. Fenno, Jr., and Professor Hugh Douglas Price for making
available to me the files they compiled in writing their own
excellent studies, "National Politics and Federal Aid to Education," written jointly by Fenno and Frank J. Munger, and
"Race, Religion, and the Rules Committee," an essay by Price
included in *The Uses of Power,* edited by Alan F. Westin. To
Joseph Hanlon, who kindly put at my disposal the library resources of the National Education Association. To the John
Simon Guggenheim Memorial Foundation, whose Fellowship
helped substantially to allow me the luxury of working on a
book without having to think of magazine articles at the same
time. To my wife, who read, criticized, typed, and put up with
my being around the house a formidably long time. And not
least to the Members of Congress, some of whom helped with
their advice and all of whom contributed in their several ways
to the rounded portrait of *political man* that is to be found in

the pages of the *Congressional Record*, that humanly contradictory thesaurus of intelligence and gibberish, information and moonshine, courage and evasion, in which an indulgent tolerance of the absurd is perhaps after all not too high a price to pay for the occasional voice of wisdom.

Contents

Preface   5

1. The Nays Have It   15
2. They All Want a School Bill, But—   32
3. Baronies and Barons   53
4. Here Lie the School Bills   74
5. Fabian Arts of the Floor   98
6. School Bills on the Floor   119
7. Domain of Howard W. Smith   140
8. No Rules for Schools   157
9. What It Would Take   190
10. First Aid for Congress   207

Index   225

Obstacle
Course
on
Capitol Hill

1

The Nays Have It

A United States Congressman has two principal functions: to make laws and to keep laws from being made. The first of these he and his colleagues perform only with sweat, patience, and a remarkable skill in the handling of creaking machinery; but the second they perform daily, with ease and infinite variety. Indeed if that government is best that governs least, then Congress is designed, by rule and tradition, to be one of the most perfect instruments of government ever devised. If, on the other hand, the world of space travel and exploding atoms has outgrown so idyllic an approach to government, then the ponderousness of Congress and its unwavering accent on the negative are as quaint as the snuffboxes that remain intact in the Senate chamber, along with the inkwells and sand bottles on the desks of the members. In either case the truth remains that for sheer difficulty the way of a serious legislative proposal through Congress is equalled only by that of a camel through the eye of a needle or a rich man into the Kingdom of God.

To anyone but a hardened political scientist, turning a bill into a law is not to be explained by comparing the process to anything so humdrum as the routine, say, of the British Parliament. It recalls, rather, those beloved but nerve-racking board games of our childhood in which a series of perils had to be survived before one's counter could be brought safely home. According to a throw of the dice or a number spun on a dial, a player would advance his counter along a winding and colorfully pictured path until it landed on a space bearing some such legend as "Fall in Pigsty, Back Ten Spaces" or "Attacked by Pirates, Lose Two Turns," the variations in hazard depending on whether his particular version of the game called for getting rabbits into a cabbage patch or locating buried treasure. The obstacles were numerous and frustrating, and just as one prayerfully approached the end of the journey, he was sure to confront the greatest danger of all, a space just short of the goal bearing some such inscription as "Caught in Bear Trap, Start Over."

The course of a bill through Congress is precisely this sort of peril-strewn path, and when a bill's sponsor is caught in a bear trap, he is likewise doomed to start over, because the next Congress will convene with a perfectly blank page, as though no word of his proposal had ever before been spoken. Four fat volumes of committee hearings may be in print to attest to the contrary, as well as hundreds of pages of the *Congressional Record* filled with ringing debate, but they count for nothing. He has it all to do over again, with appalling labor and the prospect of this time landing on a wholly different set of hazards.

Before we examine these in detail it may be useful to stand off and survey the game board as a whole, to catch a simultaneous glimpse of this mountain range of obstacles which one critic has described as "so formidable that they might well have been devised by men who hated the thought that legislation would ever be enacted."

To the eye of the layman the first hazard is completely invisible. In his innocence he is likely to think that a bill dropped into the hopper by his Congressman, who we will say is a newcomer, has as much chance of success as anyone else's bill. It does not. In fact, unless it is one of those hundreds of private bills that Congressmen bring in for the relief of individual constituents,[1] it has no chance at all: it has been introduced by the wrong member.

In theory all Congressmen are equal, but in practice George Orwell's formula prevails: some are more equal than others. It is not merely Nature that so ordains, though she does, of course, distribute abilities with as uneven a hand among Senators and Representatives as among any other of her creatures. Beyond Nature, there is tradition, specifically the tradition that in the making of Congressmen, as in the making of wine and hard cheese, aging is vital to the process.

In the words of Speaker Champ Clark, "A new Congressman must begin at the foot of the class and spell up." Until he has reached an advanced tenure, which he is much more likely to attain if he has a one-party constituency than otherwise, any bills of substance he may introduce are as good as dead from the moment he brings them in; for they will not be taken seriously in committee, where the real work of Congress is done. If our member has a proposal of merit and urgency,

---

[1] These petty claims take up a good part of the House of Representatives' attention on the first and third Tuesday of each month. On a given day they ranged from an award to a Louisiana postal clerk for overdue salary to a $1,000 settlement to a Missouri woman for "inconvenience and disruption incident to the crash of a B-47 aircraft" on her farm. Repeated attempts have been made to relieve Congress of this misplaced burden, but few members care to abandon a service so rich in voting appeal.

he must persuade a senior to introduce it, particularly a committee chairman or ranking minority member. Mr. Smith, going to Washington for the first time, is free to introduce a fistful of bills every day of the session, and no one will stop him. But none will ever come to a vote, much less to passage—and that will perhaps be only the least undesirable consequence of his indiscreet behavior.

Even among the veterans an unwise choice of sponsors can doom a measure in advance. A Democratic Senator promoting a socially advanced sort of bill usually tries to get a few Republican or Southern Democratic colleagues to join him as cosponsors, the hope being that a touch of respectability will serve as a lubricant. Conversely, a bill to curb trade unions, let us say, will do better for having the cosponsorship of one or two recognizable liberals. Among the most notable coups in the way of broad sponsorship was the Wagner-Ellender-Taft bill, which introduced the Federal government into public housing under the unbeatable auspices of a champion New Dealer, a bona fide States Rights' Democrat, and the acknowledged chief of conservative Republicans.

Let us say that our bill, then, has been launched under senior and tactically sound auspices. It is now ready for the second of what can turn out to be twenty-eight separate steps on the board—if it lasts that long.[2]

Since, for the most part, the fate of a bill is often fixed and sealed by the committee that gets hold of it, it is clearly important to see that a path is picked leading to the most favorably disposed of the several committees that might have

[2] Hubert Humphrey had not long been a member of the Senate when he made the discovery that there are that many stages in the enactment of a law and that "at each stage on the legislative highway a few legislators can lurk, like the pirates of Tripoli, and take toll of the passing traffic. . . ."

jurisdiction. A bill to repeal a tax on butter substitutes, for example, could logically be sent by the Speaker to either the Ways and Means Committee or the Committee on Agriculture. Ways and Means might pass it without difficulty, but Agriculture, chaired, let us say, by a dairy-state Representative, would suffocate it in the darkest pigeonhole on Capitol Hill. For this particular counter landing on that particular space, the instructions might well read, "Lose All Further Turns." When President Kennedy sent his civil rights bill to Congress in 1963, astute lieutenants in the Senate actually went to the length of introducing its most controversial section twice. This provision, to enforce desegregation of privately owned hotels, stores, theaters and other public accommodations, was incorporated in the general bill but was believed to have no chance of surviving Senator Eastland's Judiciary Committee. In addition, therefore, it was introduced as a separate measure, presumably affecting interstate commerce, so that it could be routed to the floor by way of Senator Magnuson's much friendlier Commerce Committee.

As a rule, however, *all* committees are regarded as burial grounds, and there is usually not much to choose. A bill has only one chance in ten to come out of any of them alive, much less intact. Indeed, having now got his counter to that stretch of the board labeled "In Committee," the player soon realizes that *any* move he makes can be fatal. For it is the function and duty of these thirty-six standing committees—twenty in the House and sixteen in the Senate—to thin a roaring torrent of bills down to a manageable trickle. And here let us give credit where it is due. With 535 members, each bringing in an average of twenty bills a year, either Congress as a whole or, worse still, the country, would be buried under a landslide of legislation were it not for these great sifters. As things work out, it is the legislation that is buried instead—90 percent of all that is introduced. Even of the remaining 10 percent, much less than half is ultimately passed by both houses and signed into law. And a good thing, too.

But to grant the necessity of this gigantic screening process is not to say that the sifting is necessarily done with discrimination or even with regard for the wishes of the majority. All too often the reverse is true. Along with hundreds of harebrained proposals, serious and important legislation has been snuffed out in committee, session after session, without ever being given a chance to come to the floor for a vote. A glaring example is the perennial attempt to give the inhabitants of Washington the normal right of adults to manage their municipal affairs. Since 1948 the Senate has five times passed such home-rule bills, once by the lopsided vote of 61 to 22, but each time companion bills vanished without a trace in the House Committee for the District of Columbia. Sometimes hearings were held and sometimes that ritual was dispensed with, but in no case was the House of Representatives allowed to vote on the question.[3]

All bills referred to a committee are supposed, at least by the naïve, to get some kind of consideration. But if the chairman—these, as we shall see, are the great oligarchs of the system—chooses to ignore a measure, it usually stays ignored. He can put off hearings as long as the spirit moves him, or decline to hold them at all; he can keep the bill off his agenda, which he rigidly controls, until the session is all but over and floor action is no longer possible; or he can adjourn committee meetings repeatedly for lack of a quorum, which he can usu-

---

[3] Seeking an explanation, the social scientist might reasonably note that more than half of the majority party's members on the Committee, including the chairman, are Southerners, with little enthusiasm for home rule in a capital city now 54 percent Negro. Whatever the motive, the fact is that a Congress with cosmic problems in its lap must still find time to consider local ordinances regulating the sale of fish, permitting school teachers to spank unruly pupils, changing street names, and authorizing more dogs for the Police Force Canine Corps.

ally arrange. But the simplest and most common procedure, by far, is to use his majority on the committee (and he has powerful means of persuasion) simply to table the referred bill. Almost invariably this means to kill it for the life of the Congress.

Even when a committee decides to report a bill to the floor, it may have so "marked up," or amended, the measure that it has to be completely redrawn. The new version is then reported out as a "clean bill," though from the original sponsor's standpoint the adjective may seem wildly inappropriate. He may, on the other hand, be pleased with the committee's work or at least recognize that his creation now has a possible chance where it had none before. But if he is not pleased, he can only try painfully to erase the amendments on the floor one by one, or disown his disfigured brainchild altogether.

If a committee does report a bill, the chances are that it will report it favorably, since it is much easier to table it quietly than to go to the trouble of making an adverse report. But does committee approval mean that the sponsor's troubles are over? Not at all. It merely means that his counter proceeds to the Rules Committee, the next hazard on the board—and one of the deadliest.

Since, in spite of their cavalier ways, many more bills are reported out by the committees than Congress can possibly consider, someone has to decide which ones will be brought to the floor and which will be left pending until they wither away. First come, first served is obviously not the principle to apply when a batch of freshly reported measures may include one bill to meet a dire defense emergency, one to appropriate funds for sending a man to the moon, and another to designate Slimy Creek Dam hereafter as Jesse James Dam in honor of a local celebrity. In the Senate the power to fix priorities rests with the majority party leaders, which is fair enough since the party in control is judged by the legislative results it produces. But in the House of Representatives the job falls to the Committee on Rules, which has over the years turned a discretionary power into a far-reaching control over the whole legislative process. Having no responsibility to the electorate, which hardly knows it exists, or to the leadership, which bears a relationship to it something like that of Dr. Frankenstein to his monster, the Rules Committee is free to give a bill a green light or not. Its actions seem often to depend on how its majority, or even just its chairman, is moved at the moment by personal prejudice, politics, or mere whim.

Not only does Rules decide on the fateful order of business, but it can dictate how long a bill is to be debated on the floor, which Congressmen will manage the debate, whether and to what extent the bill may be further amended, and even some of the parliamentary procedure to be employed. What is more astonishing, the chairman of Rules has been known to return a bill to the committee that has already approved it and to demand substantive changes as the price of sending it to the floor.

Obviously not everyone in the House is concerned over what appears to be at the least a remarkable concentration of power, and the Rules Committee has its defenders—to be heard from in a later chapter. In truth, the vital job it has to do does call for evaluation of a subtle sort, and no matter how it decides between conflicting claims to priority, it is going to come in for criticism. Even its demand for substantive changes in a bill can be defended on the ground that it may have reason to believe that a bill has no chance without such change and would therefore only clog the legislative flow.

Nevertheless, the fact remains that the Rules Committee is a first-class hazard to any measure. The annals of Congress are filled with instances of historic legislation smothered in

Rules for years before finally being blasted out by extraordinary pressure—minimum wage, housing, aid to depressed areas, civil rights, and Alaskan and Hawaiian statehood among modern instances. Howard W. Smith, who has presided over Rules since 1955, has been known to disappear rather than call a meeting if the pressure is on him to pass along a bill he would rather see stifled. At a crucial moment in the fight to release a civil rights bill in 1957 he left town, explaining on his return that he had had to inspect a barn that burned down on his Virginia farm. Speaker Sam Rayburn, who for all his power was almost as helpless as any other member when it came to the Rules Committee, merely observed: "I knew Howard Smith would do most anything to block a civil rights bill, but I never suspected he would resort to arson."

To add a little spice to the game, ways *have* been provided to slip one's counter past an adverse Rules Committee—but the navigation called for is hardly easier than that of Odysseus easing his ship between Scylla and Charybdis. Complaints about the tyranny of Rules are invariably met with the reply that for a majority of the House to "work its will" it need only petition to have a bill discharged—and at a glance nothing seems simpler. A petition is placed on the Speaker's desk, and as soon as it is signed by 218 members, a bare majority of the membership, a motion is immediately in order to dislodge the bill in question from any committee that has been keeping it bottled up, including Rules. Presumably, if a majority have signed the petition, a majority will vote for the motion. What could be fairer?

Yet resort to petition is extremely rare, and success is even rarer. The reason for this is not, as defenders of the status quo sometimes suggest, that the Rules Committee unerringly anticipates the will of the majority. On the contrary, when the procedure was used to pry out the Wages and Hours bill in 1938, the required signatures were rounded up in two hours and twenty minutes. No, the reason it is so seldom invoked is that such pressure is considered distasteful, difficult, and politically dangerous unless the top party leadership in the House is ardently behind it. This it rarely is, because the committee chairmen are part of the leadership and, on this score at least, they are inclined to stick together.

For an individual member to antagonize a powerful committee chairman is to jeopardize his standing in a body that can be notoriously hard on lone wolves. A Representative will think long before originating a discharge petition or even signing one when he knows that the move may eventually cost him influential support for future bills, especially those private bills and pork-barrel projects that Congressmen thrive on politically; without which, in fact, they do not long remain on Capitol Hill.

It is only after all this deadly preliminary byplay has been endured, and survived, that the fight for a bill comes into the public view. Even then only the tiniest fraction of the public follows the struggle in a general way, through the press, and a much smaller fraction understands what is actually happening. At best, observing a legislative battle on the floor is rather like watching a football game; a flashy end run can be appreciated from the grandstand, but a knowledge of what goes on the rest of the time is confined largely to coach, referee, and some, but not all, of the players.

Sudden death on the floor is not common for important bills, but it has happened, especially to bills that have been reported out by a committee with only thin or grudging support, and it can come in several ways. When all amendments are in, a member may move to recommit, that is, to send the bill back to committee for further consideration. Usually this is nothing more than a discreet method for killing a bill while professing to want it improved. At best, to return to our board-game figure, the move means "Back Ten Spaces." If adjournment is approaching, the result is as happily fatal as an adverse vote and not nearly so revealing in the voting record.

In the devious course of amending a measure on the floor, when no decisive vote is expected and many members are back in their offices, sudden death can strike in the form of a freak motion. An opponent, recognized for an amendment, blandly moves to "strike the enacting clause." If passed, the effect of his motion is to remove the phrase with which all bills begin: "Be it enacted by the Senate and House of Representatives . . ." Since without this vital bit of wordage, all that follows would be as meaningless as a New Year's resolution, the bill is quickly pronounced dead and carried out for interment.

Much more the rule than these swift and dramatic fatalities, however, is a kind of slow dissolution and sometimes lingering death. In the nature of things, lawmaking by 535 individuals is bound to compel a certain degree of dilution, and if that were the sole purpose of amendments, nothing could be said against the process. But at times the erosion goes so far that the tired proponents of a bill are reduced in the end to voting for it only as a matter of form and with no conviction that it will ever do what it was designed for. It was in this weary spirit that Senator Barkley remarked of the Full Employment bill, after it had gone through the Senate sawmill, that it "promised anyone needing a job the right to go out and look for one."

With more subtlety, opponents of a measure may bring in, or at least support, amendments ostensibly designed to strengthen it but so extreme that moderates who might have voted for the measure are turned implacably against it. Congressmen have been known to vote for an amendment that they would normally abhor, simply because they knew it would cause waverers to join with them in voting down the whole bill. This is one reason why voting records are not an infallible guide.

An extreme form of this technique is to kill a bill by attaching an objectionable "rider." Normally these are irrelevant proposals tacked onto bills in the belief that they will thus have an easier chance of passage than if they had to go through the mill on their own. But the purpose just as often is to attach a millstone that can be counted on to sink the measure. Most state legislatures have long since outlawed the rider, but, except in connection with appropriation bills, it survives in Congress as a hardy relic from a cruder day. Mark Twain encountered the practice when he tried to get legislative help to protect authors from literary theft. "See here," he asked Speaker Joseph Cannon, "does every fellow who comes here get hitched up to a train he does not want to pull?"

If a player has got his counter past all the dangers so far mentioned, he can breathe easier, but not much easier. He is still less than halfway home. Passed by the House of Representatives, the bill is now ready to go through a like series of strainers in the Senate. Possibly a similar, or even identical, measure has already been launched on the Senate side, but whether it was introduced at the same time or only after the House passed it, the obstacle course is much the same. It is referred to a committee, which has all the standard alternatives. It can quietly bury the bill or it can turn it over to a subcommittee for protracted hearings, at which the same witnesses who appeared before the House committee will give exactly the same testimony, spending the same amount of time all over again and filling duplicated volumes of printed transcript, all at the public cost.

Then, again, the Senate committee may turn the bill into something unrecognizable to either its original authors *or* to the House committee that has chewed over it in its own fashion. When a bill emerges from a Senate committee in *any* form, it waits for scheduling on the pleasure of the Majority Leader, who will, when he thinks the time right, move that the Senate take it up, regardless of its numerical place on the calendar.

At this point a variation occurs. A majority may be willing to take up the bill, but if it is one that is passionately opposed by even a small minority, it can be doomed by the Senate's peculiar contribution to parliamentary practice, the filibuster. A determined band—"a little group of wilful men," as President Wilson called the filibusters of his day—can talk even on the motion to bring up the controversial bill. And they can go on talking, to the exclusion of all other Senate business, until such time as the author of the motion surrenders or until two-thirds of the entire membership votes to close debate. Should this drastic sanction of "cloture" be invoked and the bill itself brought to debate, the filibusters may then start all over again. But so great is the reluctance of Senators to silence each other, even after weeks of talk, that cloture is as rare in the chamber as physical assault. The attempt in 1962, against a band of liberal filibusters rather than the usual Southern practitioners, was the first to succeed in thirty-five years.

Apart from this high wind, the dangers of the Senate floor are roughly the same as those encountered in the House. There are the same possibilities for sudden death, for recommittal, for amendments that weaken a bill and for amendments that deliberately strengthen it so much that its moderate supporters turn against it.

George Washington is supposed to have expounded to Jefferson on one occasion his view of a bicameral Congress as a system in which hot, or ill-considered legislation from the people's representatives in the House could be poured "into the senatorial saucer to cool it." It is no longer easy to say which chamber is the cup and which the saucer, but often enough they do serve as a check on each other. Sometimes Representatives, and even the House leadership, will let a bill get through that is palpably unworkable and loaded with contradictory amendments, counting heavily on the Senate to bury it. On the other hand, Senate leaders have been known to let a bill languish in committee or die on the Calendar, defending their indifference on the ground that since the companion bill has no chance of emerging from the House Rules Committee, there is no use wasting the Senate's time with it. Occasionally even the subdued rivalry between the two bodies flares up at the expense of urgently needed legislation. A feud between chairmen of the House and Senate Appropriations Committees, both octogenarians, blocked billions of dollars toward the end of the Eighty-seventh Congress, threatening within a month to leave no agency of government with a nickel on which to operate.

While such open clashes between the houses are rare, differences between them on particular bills are frequent and inevitable. They are also one of the major hazards in the game. When the differences are minor, sponsors in either House may simply move the acceptance of the other chamber's version, and if they succeed, the deed is done. But when the differences are substantial—in some cases one may be a complete substitute for the other, differing in everything but the "Be it enacted" clause—then the job of reconciling must be left to a conference committee, composed of members from the appropriate standing committees of each House. Before a conference committee can be appointed and get to work, however, a resolution must be voted on to that effect, and when our counter gets to this point in the House, the player may again

observe a sign reading: "Danger—Rules Committee Ahead."
For it is that old acquaintance, probably depicted on the
board as an ogre, that now decides whether to sanction the
conference.[4] If it decides to sit on the matter until the Congress adjourns, then the bill is dead even though both houses
have already voted for it, in different versions.

Should the bill appear at last on the table of a conference
committee, the chances are good that something will come
of it; but even though both Houses are already for it in principle, the outcome is still far from certain. The House may
well have instructed its conferees that in no circumstances are
they to yield on the substance of, say, House Amendment 7,
Paragraph 2; while the Senate may just as well have laid down
the law that in no circumstances will it *accept* the substance
of House Amendment 7, Paragraph 2. If the conferees con-
clude that there is no hope of resolving such a deadlock, the
bill, after all it has been through, quietly expires in conference.

Let us say, however, that the conferees do come to terms,
splitting their differences and perhaps even working out fresh
language. Identical conference reports are then drawn up and
sent to each chamber for a vote. No amendments from the
floor are permissible at this stage, and each body is told by
its conferees that this is the best they can get, that it is this
compromise or nothing. It is still entirely possible that to a
majority of one House or the other nothing will seem the better
choice. In which case nothing is what emerges.

When both Houses of Congress have finally passed a bill,
either identical to begin with or made so by agreement, it is
printed on parchment, certified as correct by the Secretary
of the Senate and the Clerk of the House, and signed by both
the Speaker and the President of the Senate. Then all that can

---

[4] The House membership may decide *unanimously* to send the
bill to conference, in which case the Rules Committee is bypassed.
But of course any member of Rules may offer the single objection
needed to preclude unanimity, so its veto power is unaffected.

stand between it and the status of a law is a decision by the President of the United States that it is not a good bill, after all, and deserves his veto. That happens to no more than one percent of the bills passed by Congress, to be sure, but once it does, there is only an insignificant chance that the measure will be given the two-thirds vote by both houses that is required to pass it over the President's objection.

So much for the peril-strewn game on Capitol Hill. If it were no more than that, there would be in the process at least the entertainment that obstacle courses have afforded the by-stander ever since the labors of Hercules. But, not to stress the screamingly obvious, the business of Congress is not sport but the most complex, far-reaching, and urgent questions that government has ever had to face. Finance alone has so passed the limits of normal human understanding that a subcommittee chairman not long ago complained to his colleagues of the sheer impossibility of grasping a $56 billion defense bill: "I think it is probably easier for the average person to grasp the vastness of the universe than to picture this astronomical sum."

Yet the machinery with which 535 men now attempt to cope with the staggering complexities of the Atomic Age is the same machinery that served when a Congressman's mind was largely preoccupied with roads, tariffs, and free seeds for his constituents. As late as the predepression Twenties President Coolidge could remark that the Federal government could close down entirely and the average citizen wouldn't know it for three months. Despite the stunningly accelerated rate of change in the world since then, Congress pursues its plodding, ponderous ways, hardly different from the Congress of Andrew Jackson's day, except that it has acquired the barnacles of tradition.

For it is tradition, not law, that preserves some of the most criticized aspects of Congressional procedure. The Constitution provides that "Each House may determine the rules of its proceedings," but it does not require the House of Representatives to vest that power in the chairman of its Rules Committee. Nor the Senate to abide, in cases of doubt, by the wishes of a minority. Nor both chambers to subject themselves to control by men qualified solely by the passage of time. These are refinements added over the years—practical for a while, perhaps, but no longer so. And at no time sacred.

Indeed, Congress itself has made *some* changes, notably in the revolt of 1910–1911, when a rebellious House reduced the autocratic power of the Speaker, parceling it out among the committee chairmen. That was, in a sense, Runnymede, with the chairmen playing the barons to "Uncle Joe" Cannon's King John. It is enough here merely to suggest that in time the English barons, too, came in for a clipping of the wings.

2

They All Want a School Bill, But—

On a February day in 1836, Henry Clay rose in the Senate to argue for a bill that would divide among the twenty-four states the $35-million surplus that had alarmingly piled up in the United States Treasury, a problem with which the nation has since grown steadily less familiar. In the House, John Quincy Adams had for some time been proposing that such surpluses, largely the fruit of early tariff laws and the sale of Western lands, could be used by the states for general welfare purposes, including especially the building of schools, and Clay was now advancing the idea in the upper chamber against the mild opposition of Senator King of Alabama. In the indirect discourse of Gale and Seaton's *Register of Debates in Congress,* a forerunner of the *Congressional Record,* Mr. Clay is recorded as suggesting that if the Senator from Alabama were a father, "a situation in which Clay hoped to see him shortly, he would be more ready to allow the liberality of a measure which provided the means for the education of the rising generation—a liberality which every father of a family would know how to value."

Apart from the fact that $35 million in a Federal budget could still be seen with the naked eye in those days, the interesting thing about the bill was that, in spite of Clay's appeal to fatherhood, practically no one but Adams had anything quite so innocent as schools in mind. Lawmakers from New England and the Middle Atlantic states liked the proposed disbursement because they feared that if the Treasury got too healthy, it would be difficult to maintain those high tariffs to which their manufacturing constituents were already fondly devoted. Other Whiggish members favored the move out of a vague fear of having so much money piled up in the same city with President Jackson, of whom they entertained almost pathological suspicions. On the other hand, few Jacksonians in Congress cared to risk the displeasure of a state legislature back home by spurning a welcome gift of cash.

For the purposes of lawmaking it was an ideal combination of circumstances, and to no one's surprise, therefore, the bill passed both Houses by thumping majorities. When it reached Jackson's desk, moreover, the President was easily persuaded by Van Buren and other advisers that it would be unfortunate to veto such an act of generosity in an election season. In the 127 years since then, promoters of Federal aid to the schools were never again to be in so fair a position.

The surplus disappeared before it could all be distributed, and Congress rescinded the measure the following year. But as far as Federal aid to education went, and it could not have gone far, there was something both typically incidental and prophetically left-handed in the way the national legislators went about the matter. The pattern had appeared before and it was to reappear many times again. A further touch of history here is essential to the point.

A half century earlier, before the adoption of the Constitution, the Congress of the Confederation had specified that in all the vast Federal territories to be governed under the Northwest Ordinance income from lot number 16 of every township was to be used for the endowment of the community's schools. Establishing a pattern for the states of the future, the device proved of far-reaching importance in the educational development of the country—and a standing refutation of the charge that Federal concern for the schools is a modern and devilish concept of the welfare state. But we have it from more than one historian that the post-Revolutionary government, heavily in debt and in desperate need of revenue, had something more, or less, in mind than education for its own sake. "We may be reasonably assured," writes George B. German, that the committee in charge of the Ordinance "did not act . . . purely and simply from any abstract ideals of, or concrete zeal for, education. The impelling motive seems to have been more a consideration of economics than a consideration for education. . . . The Western lands furnished the only ready and common fund for the extinguishment of the Revolutionary debt. Hence there could be no objection to the incorporation into that ordinance of any reasonable provision that might accelerate the sale of public lands." Not to put too fine a point on it, the move was in part an early example of the real estate come-on.

In educational matters this indirect, behind-the-barn approach has been the course taken by the Federal government ever since. Despite a dozen false starts, gestures, and abortive attempts throughout the nineteenth century, it was not to get even faintly appreciable money into the pre-college school system [1] until twenty years ago—and then only in a spotty

---

[1] It must be kept in mind that throughout this book the concern is with Federal aid to the primary and secondary schools. Bills bearing on higher education are only incidental to the story.

fashion and by way of legislation that has ever since smelled strongly of the pork barrel. In the critical days of World War II many communities suddenly found themselves at a double disadvantage: Tax-free Federal defense installations were replacing what had been good taxpaying property, and at the same time the children of Federal employees were putting additional strain on the facilities of the local schools. By way of relief Congress passed an act allowing government contributions to the building of new schools in these "impacted" districts. The move turned out to be hugely popular with local taxpayers and therefore with their Congressmen, who presently saw no argument against extending such contributions to the maintenance and operation of schools as well as their construction.

Overnight this type of payment became an accepted fact of life, but the acceptance had more to do with a Congressman's compulsion to get his district a slice of whatever was being handed out than it did with a fondness for Federally nurtured education. In fact, Congressmen who regularly and truculently fight off attempts to pass general aid programs vote just as regularly and truculently *for* these impacted area handouts. Some 4,000 districts, accounting for a third of all public schools, now happily accept this distinct though limited form of assistance, and a Congressman can no more reject it, even where it is not needed, than he can turn down the offer of a spare bridge or an unnecessary post office. The highly solvent Maryland suburbs of Washington, for example, draw something like $2.5 million a year from the Federal Treasury simply because so many of their residents work for the government. But for some hard-pressed town in West Virginia, lacking a defense plant, the fiction must be preserved that education is strictly a local concern, happily beyond the grasping reach of Washington bureaucrats.

The truth is that in a disorganized and uncoordinated way,

those bureaucrats are now involved in the educational system of the United States to the extent of some billion and a quarter dollars a year, though only a small fraction of this finds its way to the elementary and secondary schools. Besides the investments already mentioned, and skipping lightly over such freakish Federal responsibilities as schooling the Aleutian children of the Pribilof Islands, a considerable "intervention" now goes on in the guise of national defense. Under a law rushed through in the somewhat hysteric days that followed Russia's orbiting of the first satellite, the Federal government, as we shall see, has distributed millions of dollars for improved instruction in mathematics, science, and foreign languages in primary and secondary schools as well as colleges.

Nevertheless, all such Federal action, sizable as it may seem, is more noteworthy for the precedent set than for the help rendered. Measured even against the current *outlay* for schooling, never mind the far greater need, it is insignificant in scope, specialized in purpose, and spotty in distribution. Yet bills to get really appreciable sums to the states for the general improvement of the schools have been beaten or buried or circumvented time after time—sporadically from 1870 to World War II, and since then as a monotonous feature of every session of Congress—until their periodic defeat has become almost as much a tradition as bean soup in the Capitol restaurants and free haircuts in the Senate.

At the same time a substantial and growing majority of the country seems to favor outright Federal assistance. In 1950, a study by Elmo Roper, commissioned by *Life,* reported that 65.4 percent of those who had heard about the issue were for such aid. In 1957, both Roper and Dr. George Gallup reported substantial advances in this sentiment. The Gallup Poll showed 76 percent in favor of Federal help in building new schools, with only 19 percent opposed and 5 percent pleading ignorance. Republicans were within a few percentage points of being as sold on the idea as Democrats, and favorable Catholic opinion actually ran higher than Protestant.

The Roper study showed remarkably similar results. So impressed, in fact, was Mr. Roper with the returns that his conclusions took on an unusually hortatory ring:

> The orators who declaim against too much Federal aid to education are in for a shock—the public does not agree with them . . .
>
> The answers are startling. They reveal that the public is strong for more and more Federal aid—not just for school buildings but for school teachers' salaries, and for whatever is needed to keep us abreast in our race for knowledge . . .
>
> In short, if the Federal Government were to take its courage in both hands and decide tomorrow morning that our crippling educational shortages were something for which it must now take a heavy measure of responsibility for the first time in the history of our Republic, the heavens would not fall. More people favor such a course than favor any other single one.

That year a Federal aid bill for the first time reached the floor of the House but, as we shall see at the proper time, it was to meet sudden death in one of its rarer parliamentary forms.

The discrepancy between what the country seems to want in the way of Federal aid to the schools and what Congress delivers happens admirably to illustrate some of the weaknesses of Congress, but it is both fair and essential at this point to take into account the role of the public itself in the legislative process and what might well be, on this particular issue, the public's contributory ambivalence.

Private Streams and Public Laws

The picture of important statutes streaming from the minds of Congressmen is on a level of reality with that of Athene springing full-grown from the brow of Zeus. Somewhat closer

to sober fact is the rule that the more far-reaching a law is,
the less likely it was conceived by *any* individual, in Congress
or out. Like a legend, rather, it probably started incoherently
and long ago, with no one quite certain of its origins. In his
excellent study, "Congress Makes a Law," Stephen K. Bailey
suggests a bit whimsically that sentiment for the Full Employment Act harks back to the Lord's Prayer—"Give us this day
our daily bread." In the same way one might trace certain
New Deal agriculture programs back to the farm policy of
the Joseph Administration in the days of Pharoah and perhaps
the Mann Act to Paris's transporting of Helen across the state
line of Athens. But for our purposes it will not be necessary
to go back as far as that.

A legislative idea, it might be said, starts out as a stream
trickling down a mountain side. It may just meander for a
while and dry up, never to be heard from again. Or it may
be joined here and there by other streams headed in the same
direction, in which case it eventually becomes a river and
gets on all the maps. The first eventuality obviously need not
concern us. The second might be illustrated in passing by the
Sherman Anti-Trust Act. For at least twenty years farmers
grumbled vaguely but ever more emphatically that "there
ought to be a law" to stop the railroads and grain elevators
from ganging up to rob them at prearranged prices. And
through those same years their demand for relief was gradually sharpened and refined in speeches by Populist leaders,
in learned books by economists, in tentative proposals by
politicians, in magazine articles by crusading journalists, in
the antimonopoly planks of party platforms, and in Presidential messages—until at last, after many attempts at legislative control, it emerged as the so-called Sherman Act, not
a line of which was framed by Senator Sherman. Those dis-
parate groups and forces that were for the bill, be it noted,

were *all* for it, mild as it was, reserving their enmity for "the Trusts."

Once on the books, the Sherman Act, like so many other statutes, became a target for those who would strengthen it, weaken it, or repeal it, and therefore a source of further law. Actually it had to wait until the Clayton Act came along twenty-four years later before it had real teeth, but the end result proved again what hard-bitten politicians know so well—that it is sometimes better to get a weak bill enacted into law and then rework it than to wait for the perfect bill to win acceptance.

Woodrow Wilson made the point with an interesting twist: "Legislation unquestionably generates legislation. Every statute may be said to have a long lineage of statutes behind it; and whether that lineage be honorable or of ill repute is as much a question as to each individual statute as it can be with regard to the ancestry of each individual legislator. Every statute in its turn has a numerous progeny, and only time and opportunity can decide whether its offspring will bring it honor or shame." [2]

In an immediate sense most important legislative proposals now come to Congress by way of the President and his executive departments. Since Washington, Presidents have been advising Congress on the nation's legislative needs, always constitutionally but with ever increasing enthusiasm, until in our own times Executive messages go to Capitol Hill every few weeks, on the whole range of the Administration's program. More than half the bills dropped into the hopper are now believed to originate in this way, leaving Congress with the function, not of originating laws, but of reviewing them, modifying them, or rejecting them. We have come at least

[2] From *Congressional Government* (p. 207), which Wilson wrote as a graduate student of political science, long before he was President and had occasion to feel strongly about the ancestry of Congressmen.

half way to the point where the Executive legislates and Congress vetoes, rather than the constitutional opposite.

To regard the Executive as a kind of third, and initiating, legislative chamber, however, is still to beg the question of where laws originate. For while bureaucrats and Presidential advisers may be even more inclined toward legislative delusions of grandeur than Congressmen themselves, they do not normally go to the length of recommending laws on Capitol Hill that are wholly creatures of their own imagining. On the contrary, they are probably carrying out the direct orders of the President, and the chances are that he, in turn, is fulfilling a pledge made in the preceding election campaign.

Once more, then, the trail leads back to groups of private citizens, and it is safe to say that behind every major piece of legislation, whether or not it is routed through the Executive, is to be found the propelling power of anywhere from one to a score of organizations. It is no more possible to imagine the Taft-Hartley Act without the initiative and public promotion of the National Association of Manufacturers than to conceive of Prohibition without the efforts of the Women's Christian Temperance Union and the National Anti-Saloon League, which for a time approached the status of an unofficial government.[3]

Over and over again Capitol Hill has resounded with the arguments, and responded to the desires, of determined and

[3] Justine Stuart, the biographer of the League's guiding spirit, Wayne B. Wheeler, says that his hero "controlled six Congresses, dictated to two Presidents, directed legislation in most of the states, picked the candidates for the more important elective and federal offices, held the balance of power in both Republican and Democratic parties, distributed more patronage than any dozen men, supervised a federal bureau from outside without official authority, and was recognized by friend and foe alike as the most masterful and powerful single individual in the United States." Probably nobody on either side of the school question can reasonably aspire to such glory, given the difference in public interest evoked by alcohol and education.

vocal elements in the country—numerically small elements of great financial power or elements of small financial power but impressive voting strength. In its successful drive to have a share in the government's space communications satellite program, the American Telephone and Telegraph Company beautifully exemplified the first of these sources of pressure. The second will be recognized at once by any New York, Chicago, or Philadelphia Congressman who has ever entertained a doubt as to how to vote on a civil rights bill. But not even wealth or votes will assure success if the seekers after a law persist in working at cross-purposes. Which brings us, with perfect logic, to the campaign for Federal aid to the schools.

Here the repeatedly fruitless attempts to turn the several streams of sentiment into something that could fairly be called a river demonstrate the third of our fluent possibilities: a rivulet may for a while run closely parallel to three or four others, with much hopeful burbling, only to part company as each one, easily diverted, follows its wayward course and all are lost to each other and to the cartographers.

Many groups have favored Federal aid to the country's elementary and secondary schools. Many have testified for it and promoted it. But over and over again, as the evidence will show, they saw Federal aid merely as a way of furthering something else that they wanted more; or they wanted Federal aid for its own sake but not enough to pay the inevitable price of compromise. So the streams have run their separate courses. At crucial moments, in fact, when the roar of their united waters might well have found a response in Congress, some of them have been known to turn around and flow right back up the mountain—as strange a sight in politics as it is in nature.

To be sure, this ambivalence is expressed almost entirely by regional and special interest groups, each with its special axe to grind, but it is nevertheless a legitimate and important part of the story. While it adds greatly to the difficulty of Congress in resolving the problem, however, it does not in the least *free* Congress of that obligation nor excuse its prolonged evasion. One need not take the view that it is for the people's legislative servant to tell its masters what they ought to want, but it is certainly for Congress in a matter of major importance to *reconcile* as best it can such group conflicts as those sketched below, rather than merely to reflect the differences and then agree, time after time, simply to brush the lot of them under the carpet.

The South Is for It, But—

It may be a little difficult to recall now that in the early days of agitation for Federal aid to the schools its most ardent champions were Senators from the Deep South. And with good reason. Bills for the purpose have generally called for help to the states on the basis of a formula that takes both need and resources into account, with the richer states bearing a proportionally greater share of the load. As a region the South therefore had the most to gain. A report in the mid-Forties showed that Alabama had 23,000 children in schools that had no water supply on the grounds, 50,000 in schools where hand pumps and open wells served the purpose, and 9,000 in schools that had no toilet facilities of any kind. Of the 5,000 or so school buildings in the state, more than half had no electric lights. A Georgia school official testifying in favor of Federal aid in 1945 complained of his particular county's disadvantage: "We have lost some of our top people with salaries as high as $3,000, when they were employed at still higher salaries elsewhere." Possibly as short-order cooks. One witness from Dixie summed it up crisply: "It looks like the kids is where the money ain't."

In the circumstances it is understandable that Southern members of Congress should have felt less strongly about states' rights when it came to Federal aid to the schools than in certain other matters. At any rate, Senate campaigns for the cause were led at various times from 1918 to 1954 by Georgia's Senator Hoke Smith, Mississippi's Senator Pat Harrison, Louisiana's Senator Allen J. Ellender, Arkansas' Senator John McClellan, and, most notably, Alabama's Senator Lister Hill. "I have been a member of the Senate since 1937," Ellender said in 1945, "and ever since that time some of us have been making efforts to obtain funds in order to aid States, the poor States, so they can better carry their school burden. . . . I think it is an advantage to New Jersey, it is an advantage to Pennsylvania, to see that the children of the South are educated, because these children become the citizens of New Jersey, Pennsylvania, and other states that are not so prolific in the production of children. . . ."

Then came the Supreme Court's thunderbolt in 1954, and the Dixie climate soured. Those Southerners who were not suddenly and thoroughly convinced of the deadly menace of Federal interference were still for school aid from Washington, but with a difference. Henceforth, they would have to be assured first that funds would be doled out with no regard whatever to such irrelevancies as whether or not a state was conforming to the Court's decree for integration. Some were prepared to go along only if the proposed assistance were not limited to public schools, since they hoped to circumvent the desegregation order with a school system entrusted overnight to private auspices.

The cooling of Southern enthusiasm was to show up dramatically in Congressional voting. Where the 22 Senators from the states of the former Confederacy had supported Federal aid bills in 1948–1949 by as much as 19 to 3, their support in 1961 had shrunk to 13 to 9. By then, Senator McClellan had so far forgotten his one-time enthusiasm for the scheme that he could warn his colleagues: "Do not, I say to my Southern friends, vote for this measure with any thought that the segregation issue is not involved. . . . That issue cannot be evaded. We cannot escape it. In due time it will be here to haunt us." It is worth noting, however, that on Federal handouts to impacted areas—here the segregation issue has been strictly ignored—the heirs of Jefferson Davis have been able to look the other way. They voted for these by 85 to 10 in the House in the same session that they opposed general aid by 82 to 22.

In short, the Deep South, which needs Federal assistance for its schools more desperately than any other section of the country, is for it, but only if it can be had without speeding up an inexorable process set in motion by the Supreme Court of the United States.

The NAACP Is for It, But—

Conversely, the Negro community is for Federal aid, but only if that same process is thereby speeded up. If Southern whites have good reason to want Federal aid in general, Negroes as a group have still better reason. The former states of the Confederacy have been unable to spend enough to educate their white children and unwilling to spend nearly as much on their colored children, the pre-1954 separate-but-equal doctrine notwithstanding. In 1940, for example, Arkansas was still paying out $37 a year for each white pupil (the median for all the states then was about $85), as against $14 a year for each Negro pupil. In Mississippi, always the extreme, the ratio was $52 to $7. It is not surprising, therefore, that Negro leaders have favored Federal aid ever since the Civil War, sincerely and with enthusiasm, but also with understandable reservations. Yet these same reservations have from time to time seriously divided the Federal aid camp and presented its opponents with ready ammunition for the attack.

It should be said, however, that in the years before the Court's historic decision, when the National Association for the Advancement of Colored People was asking only a "just and equitable apportionment" of Federal funds, rather than for desegregation, it found Southern statesmen just as unyielding. Moreover, when Negro leaders showed a flexibility even as to this modest demand, their reasonableness got them nowhere. In 1943, the late Senator Langer of North Dakota tried to amend a school-aid bill to provide for an equitable apportionment not only of Federal funds but also of the state funds that these would supplement. In short, he would have made sure at least that the separate facilities were equal. The NAACP generously opposed the amendment on the hard, pragmatic ground that the amendment would kill the bill— and, sure enough, it did. Clarence Mitchell, the Association's Washington representative, says that Langer never forgave the organization for failing to support him. "We were just trying to be cooperative with the other organizations supporting the bill," Mitchell plaintively explains. Neither he nor any other Negro leader would, or could possibly afford to, take so conciliatory a stand today.

The Association's position has long since hardened into insistence on a much sterner proviso, to wit, no Federal money to states still in defiance of the Supreme Court's order to integrate "with all deliberate speed." This condition, commonly called the Powell Amendment, after the sometimes militant, sometimes merely flamboyant, Representative from New York's Harlem district, does not mean that a state could not collect any Federal aid unless its schools were completely desegregated. The ban would apply only to states that retained stat-

utes forbidding desegregation or that in the judgment of the
Federal government had made no progress at all in the direction of the Court's decree.

Reasonable as this position is in theory and warranted as
it is in emotion, it has unhappily proved futile and divisive
in practice. There is no doubt that its introduction regularly
pleases opponents of Federal aid, who are thereby all but
assured of the bill's defeat. Sometimes, as we shall see,
Northern opponents anticipate Mr. Powell by introducing the
amendment themselves, thus at the same time taking credit
for solicitude concerning civil rights and neatly knifing a
measure that would benefit colored children as well as white.
Concerning one such attempt, the sophisticated Mr. Mitchell
conceded his complete mistrust of the Representative's motives
but added, "In Congress good things sometimes are done by
the wrong people for the wrong reasons."

Responsible Negro leaders who want Federal aid to the
public schools will tell you confidentially that they not only
hope not to have thrust upon them the choice between aid
with segregation and no aid at all, but that they do not expect
this to happen. The religious issue, they say, is far more explosive than the racial and is the issue that is truly blocking the
way. The conviction that responsibility lies elsewhere affords
them visible relief.

The Catholic Church Is for It, But—

Like the Southern segregationists and the NAACP, the Roman
Catholic Church has over the years undergone a considerable
change of heart with respect to Federal aid to the schools. But
where the first two groups moved from positions of total acceptance toward something much more provisional, the Church
started out in total opposition. The National Catholic Welfare
Conference, which serves as the voice of the hierarchy, was

actively against all measures for Federal aid to the schools until the early 1940s. As much as any devotees of states' rights, church leaders regarded education as peculiarly the province of state and local government, and they feared and mistrusted the intrusion of Federal power in the area. It had been hard enough to put up with state-sanctioned readings from the Protestant Bible without taking a chance on what Washington officials might impose as a consequence of Federal aid.

By the mid-1940s, however, circumstances had changed drastically. Depression and then war would have left an enormous backlog of needed school construction, even if the increase in enrollment had been merely steady. Instead it was staggering. Where only one out of twenty American children had attended parochial schools in 1900, about one in twelve were so enrolled when Father William E. McManus appeared before the Senate Committee on Education and Labor in 1942 to support a bill that would have extended Federal aid to parochial as well as public schools. "Heretofore," noted Senator Walsh with mild surprise, "the Catholic Welfare Council has opposed legislation concerning Federal aid." Far from opposing it in principle, thereafter, the bishops as a group were to favor it, provided the parochial schools were included, and Federal aid bills were repeatedly to be brought in by Catholics in good standing.

Justification lay in the emergency which, as it turned out, was to be of a continuing nature. Since Father McManus' appearance, pressures on the Catholic educational system have increased phenomenally. Of the roughly 42 million children now in the elementary and secondary grades of the nation's schools, some 5.5 million, or more than an eighth, attend these parochial schools, which could almost double their elementary enrollment without exhausting the supply of Catholic children. In New York City, one pupil in three attends a Catholic school, and in Pittsburgh every other child. Moreover, just when teachers were needed in greater numbers than ever, the free, or almost free, supply from the religious orders seemed to be drying up. Whether the orders were attracting fewer young men and woman or whether those who were attracted shied away from teaching, more and more lay teachers had to be brought into the system. Since 1920 their number has increased some eight times, until they now represent about one third of the country's parochial school faculty. While their average salary ($3,500) is far below the public school average ($5,215) it is so far above what is paid back to a religious order for the services of a nun, priest, or brother as to leave the parochial budget-makers with a staggering problem.

Given the need for expanding plant, the problem of holding lay teachers against the lure of public school salaries, and pressure from Catholic parents to raise standards, the Church is no longer thinking merely of emergency aid, such as it has received indirectly through the loan provisions of the National Defense Education Act. Bishops and cardinals are still to be found who decry *all* Federal aid, but the shift in emphasis is clearly visible in the distance traveled between Cardinal Spellman in 1949 and Monsignor Frederick G. Hochwalt, speaking for the NCWC in 1961. Said Cardinal Spellman on the earlier occasion: "We are not asking for general public support of religious schools. Under the Constitution, we do not ask nor can we expect public funds for the construction or repair of parochial school buildings, or for the support of teachers or for other maintenance costs." By 1961 the Council was seeking low-cost loans for classroom construction, and when President Kennedy called such loans unconstitutional, Monsignor Hochwalt bluntly announced a shift in strategy: "If loans and grants are on the same constitutional basis," he said, "we are asking for grants. The Government has opened the door on the question of constitutionality all the way." The bishops had already made it their formal position that unless parochial schools were somehow included in the aid program, "there will be no alternative but to oppose such discrimination."

Was it just the emergency that pushed the hierarchy to this extreme position? At press conferences President Kennedy several times seemed puzzled that the religious issue, so long quiescent in the debate over Federal aid to the schools, should have flared up so sharply in his Presidency. The explanation, Daniel P. Moynihan suggested in *The Reporter*, besides sheer need, lay in the strong probability that with the Democrats again in power, impressive Federal aid to the schools would at long last be voted into law. The occasion would be an historic landmark, and it was vital that the parochial school system be given a share from the very outset, before reinforced tradition as well as competition could plunge it into a permanently inferior status.

Separationists and Others Are for It, But—

Under this head are both those for whom separation of church and state is an incidental principle, and those for whom it is the driving force and reason for being. Protestants and Others United for Separation of Church and State is probably the most articulate of the second of these groups, and its course is clear. Warning of "intercreedal bitterness" should the wall of separation be breached, its associate director once read to a Congressional committee a passage from the *Christian Century* by way of evidence: "We will oppose the enactment of laws which require such payments [to support Catholic schools]. If Congress is pressured into enacting such laws, we will contest them in the courts. If the courts reverse themselves and declare such laws constitutional, we will still refuse to pay these taxes. . . ."

Representing the less extreme and more influential National

Council of the Churches of Christ in America, Dr. Gerald E.. Knoff, was almost as unequivocal: "If Roman Catholic leaders raise their demand as a moral issue, Protestant leaders must reply that they oppose the proposal as a moral issue." And from this stand the opposition of religious groups shades off through varying degrees of objection from the Lutheran Church, the Jewish religious community (except for some of its Orthodox segments), the Presbyterians, Unitarians, Methodists, Baptists, Seventh Day Adventists, and Mormons, not necessarily in descending order of feeling on the subject.

Representatives of all these denominations, and of others, have urged measures to inject Federal funds into the veins of the public school system. But none is ready to have them at the price of Federal help to parochial schools as well—even though at least three of them have impressive parochial school systems of their own.

Among the incidential separatists may be classed some of the professional education groups, most notably the National Education Association, which ranks high among the big lobbies of the capital. More than any other single organization, the NEA, with a membership of over 700,000 teachers, has been the champion of Federal aid, its zeal in the cause going far back in its 106 years of history. But it leaves no doubt whatever concerning the "but" it reserves on the question. At its Representative Assembly in Denver in 1962, the NEA took occasion to "reaffirm its long-standing policy," one of its organs reported, "that the Congress should give priority to appropriating funds to be used by the states *only* for the support of *tax-supported* public elementary and secondary schools." The italics are the publication's, which continued: "The Association believes that the American tradition of separation of church and state should be consistently and forthrightly safeguarded. The application of this principle to education at all

levels in keeping with the letter and spirit of national and
state constitutions is sound public policy."

So fixed is the NEA's position in the matter of separation
that when Congress was on the point of voting construction
grants to private as well as state-supported colleges, including
those under religious auspices, the Association raised a hue
and cry against the bill. From its headquarters telegrams
went out to every member of Congress warning that the grant
provision "imperials America's traditional concept of separation of church and state," and the bill died on the spot.

In its opposition on this occasion the NEA was joined by
the American Association of School Administrators, the National Congress of Parents and Teachers, and the Council of
Chief State School Officers. On the other hand, the American
Federation of Teachers, which mildly opposed aid to parochial
schools in the past, has gradually come to favor it—partly because it is genuinely convinced there is no other way to get
Federal aid for *any* schools, partly because it has a high percentage of Catholic members, and partly because it generally
finds it irksome to cooperate with the somewhat competitive
NEA, which it has been known to regard at times as a "company union."

Besides its conditional supporters, Federal aid to the schools
has had, of course, its full share of unconditional opponents.
Led by the United States Chamber of Commerce, they usually include the National Grange, the Daughters of the American Revolution, the Investment Bankers Association of America, and, at least in recent years, the American Legion. But for
the moment it is enough to say of these that their all-out hos-
tility has probably been less damaging to the cause than the
failure of its supporters to present anything like a solid front.

The streams of opinion that favor Federal aid have simply
failed to merge. Each group has been so bent on going its own

way and no other that Congress is afforded at least an explanation for its prolonged failure to act. But to explain is by no means to justify. We return now to Capitol Hill to see with what difficulty the machinery works even in simple circumstances, where there is no problem of reconciling sharp differences or painfully building a consensus.

3

Baronies and Barons

In any democratic country other than the United States, it is easy to find out at the beginning of a session what the national legislature proposes to do. Quite simply, the program of the majority is the program of the chief of government, call him prime minister, premier, chancellor, or grand vizier. Either it is enacted, by and large, or one of two things happens: he and his cabinet gracefully pack up and go home, or the voters elect a new parliament. In either case, executive and legislature are soon back in tandem and the immediate legislative future is again predictable.

In the United States, by contrast, the executive enjoys security of tenure, limited though it is, but his program has no security at all. It is useless to ask him about the chances of enacting a Federal aid to education bill or any other bill because he can no more predict Congressional behavior than he can predict the stock market's, even though his partisans may be in nominal control of Congress—and indeed owe that control to the fact that his magic name on the ballot swept many of them into office.

Neither will it do much good to ask the Speaker of the House, the Majority Leader of the Senate, or the party whips what their colleagues will deliver. They have plans, of course, but they know all too well that success depends on the will or whim of thirty-six standing committees—or, more particularly, of thirty-six committee chairmen. Senator Mike Mansfield, currently the Majority Leader and a mild-mannered man, described the situation with wistful accuracy: "I'm not the leader, really. They don't do what I tell them. I do what they tell me." And by way of elaboration, he added, "We've had a dispersal of responsibility. How can I know everything that's going on? The brains are in the committees."

Mansfield's explanation was perhaps overly modest—and overly careful about the sensibilities of the committee barons—but as to their power it was neither new nor exaggerated. Addressing himself to the same theme three quarters of a century before, Woodrow Wilson observed that "the House has as many leaders as there are subjects of legislation" and each standing committee "goes its own way at its own pace" without unity, method, or common purpose. Both houses, he thought, conducted their affairs by "an odd device of disintegration."

They did then and they do now. As the Eighty-eighth Congress warmed up in January of 1963, Senator Harry F. Byrd, an implacable opponent of President Kennedy's tax program, blandly announced that his Finance Committee would be too busy to report that top-priority measure, the most urgent on the Administration's list, until after Labor Day. The Majority Leader and the President's other chief lieutenants in Congress might have been expected to clear the track for so major a piece of legislation, but no, its fate had to be left to the hostile

chairman of one of those committee mills that "grind slowly,
yet they grind exceeding small." In the same way, autocratic
preparations for the session went forward in the other baronies
on the Hill. The Administration's worries did not revolve about
such questions as whether or not a House or Senate majority
could be obtained for this or that item of its program. They
revolved rather about the question of whether a bevy of committee chairmen, all nominally of the Administration party,
would deign to let much of the President's program even get
to the House or Senate floor. Their concern proved to have
been thoroughly warranted.

The young Wilson, looking at Congress with a fresh eye,
exaggerated only mildly when he made the point that "The
House sits, not for serious discussion, but to sanction the conclusions of its committees. . . . It legislates in its committee
rooms; not by the determinations of majorities, but by the
resolutions of specially commissioned minorities." As a result,
much of an Administration's program never even reaches the
stage of debate. Indeed it has been reliably calculated that
20 percent of President Kennedy's legislative requests to the
Eighty-seventh Congress received no consideration whatever,
either in committee or on the floor, an affront uniquely flowing
from our systematic separation of powers. So groggy was that
particular Congress rendered by committee waywardness that
the *New York Times* was moved to reflect that "The 87th
could not even find the exit without stumbling." The 88th, it
was to turn out, could hardly find the entrance.

Yet the sheer need of a committee system as such, of divid-
ing a cumbersome 535-man body into small working groups,
is too obvious to question or to call for extended argument.
The individual member cannot conceivably master the whole
range of subjects that come up for legislation or even acquire
a respectable smattering of knowledge about more than a
very few of them. This is especially true since, as several mem-

bers themselves have testified, as much as 80 percent of their time is drained away on nonlegislative work. As his constituents' "errand boy," a Congressman may on a given day help one of them get a government loan and explore job possibilities for two others. He arranges for a fourth to see the right man in the Pentagon about the purchase of surplus goods and for a fifth to see someone else about patenting an invention. He talks with a reporter or two about a bill he has just introduced and arranges for a delegation of housewives from the district to make a special tour of Washington and Mt. Vernon. (Constituents are not above asking their Congressmen even to make hotel reservations for them.) In the course of the day he meets another delegation from home to talk about prospects for a new Federal courthouse and probably signs seventy-five to a hundred letters to other constituents who have favored him with requests or advice and all of whom expect at least a personally signed reply. It is too much to ask that in the remaining 20 percent of his time he become expert in international finance, nuclear testing, technological unemployment, farm surpluses, race relations, Latin American affairs, and medical care for the aged, not to mention taxation, the national debt, outer space, mass transportation, and the preservation of world peace.

Since all these matters are likely to come up in any session of a contemporary Congress, it is not to be wondered at that the average member pursues the specialties of his own committee or two, and for the rest takes on faith the views of his party colleagues on the various other committees. Presumably they have sat in on hearings and heard the real experts, taken part in the discussions, and had a hand in either the majority or minority report. The floor debate is managed by these two groups from the committee, and it is rare that a bill meets effective opposition on the floor that is not led by someone who first fought it within the committee itself.

The point is worth noting, too, that in spite of the ever-increasing initiative of the Executive Branch in proposing legislation, Congress is still a lawmaking body in a way that most parliaments are not. Important bills that come before its British counterpart, for example, are all drawn up by the government, and Parliament for the most part accepts, rejects, or modifies. Its members have neither desks nor even offices to speak of, and they are subjected to far less pressure for personal services to their constituents.[1]

Given the undisputed need of a committee system, why the complaints about it inside Congress and out? Why should so restrained and cool a member as Senator Joseph Clark of Pennsylvania rise on the floor to castigate the "Senate Establishment" as the "antithesis of democracy" and a "self-perpetuating oligarchy," an almost unheard of assault to make within the hallowed precincts of what Senators have for a hundred years thought of as The Club? And why should the scholarly Senator Paul Douglas thereupon get up to praise the courage of his colleague? "We are not supposed to talk

[1] Lest we get too carried away by sympathy for Congressmen, however, it may be noted that a Member of Commons draws only £1,750 a year, including expenses, which often come to more than the salary itself. Peers get only expenses for attending, a maximum of three guineas a day. A Member of Congress, on the other hand, is currently rewarded for his efforts at $22,500 a year, plus an allotment to pay the salaries of a staff (a Senator will have twelve or fifteen employees), a suite of offices (five rooms for Senators, two for Representatives), free mailing privileges and a healthy allowance for telegrams and telephone, medical care and hospitalization at even lower rates than "socialized medicine" could offer, office expenses in his home district, and world-wide travel at the public expense. To sweeten the arrangement further, he may also count on special prices for radio recordings, TV movies of himself in action, and the mimeographing of his speeches. He also gets $1,800 for stationery, free flowers for his office from a nearby government greenhouse, and, in the case of Senators, free haircuts. The perquisites of a Member of Commons are confined to transportation to and from Parliament, free telephoning limited to local London calls, and forty-eight sheets of House of Commons writing paper a day, twenty-four large and twenty-four small, with envelopes.

about it because we might offend someone or might indicate
that matters are decided in a different way from the way they
are discussed in public. In short, we should not call attention
to the nakedness of the emperor."

Of those criticisms that have from time to time been made,
and found so unpalatable to the Congressional taste, the first
has been touched on in Chapter I—the arbitrary power of a
committee not merely to recommend rejection of a bill, but
to forbid its even being considered by the rest of the Congress,
no matter how important, or urgent, or desired by the general
population. It was not the 87th Congress that rejected President Kennedy's proposal for medical care for the aged; it was
the House Ways and Means Committee, by a margin of five
votes. By one vote the same committee refused to let the
House pass on an extension of unemployment compensation,
already approved by the Senate. In the same way a subcommittee of Banking and Currency decided, after two years of
extensive hearings, that the Senate should not vote on a simple
proposal to force lending companies to tell their customers
what they were being charged by way of interest. And we
have already noted how the Committee on the District of
Columbia has for twelve years kept the House from voting
on home rule for Washington, although the Senate five times
passed bills to provide it. On what might ironically be called
the positive side, when the almighty Appropriations Committee brings in its finished product, calling for expenditures of
some *forty billion dollars,* the measure goes through the House
with a whoop and a holler, no amendments allowed and no
voice lifted in dissent.

Even more of a target for critics than the arbitrary power
of the committees is the arbitrary power of the chairmen
thereof. A major committee gets hundreds of bills in the course
of a session, and somebody has to decide on an order of im-

portance. That someone is, perhaps logically, the chairman, but to justify present practice on this ground would be naïve beyond the limits of tolerance. All too often, importance has far less to do with the priority assigned a bill than the chairman's purely personal reaction to it. Former Senator Burton K. Wheeler, as tough a Congressional operator as any and more candid than most, has made perfectly clear his own concept of the role of a committee chairman:

> I felt I could make my contribution by blocking bad bills as well as pushing good ones. Twice during my chairmanship the House approved bills to legalize wire tapping, under certain conditions. Twice I saw to it that the House-passed bill was referred to our [Senate] Interstate Commerce Committee —rather than to Judiciary, where it might have gone—and twice I sat on the bill, that is, never let it come up for a vote.

Whatever the rules of a particular committee, it is not hard for the chairman, in practice, to have his own way with the agenda. It is he who has the preliminary look at the bills referred to his committee, and when he announces that "We will now consider H. R. 179," he has an undoubted advantage over his colleagues, who have probably not yet heard of H. R. 179, much less read it.

Yet, clearly, timing is of the essence; since only a small fraction of bills and resolutions can possibly come to the floor, the power to choose some is the power to doom others. More subtly, it is the power to make the clearing of a bill dependent on the inclusion of features that appeal to the chairman and the elimination of those that do not. In the Truman Administration Representative Doughton of North Carolina, then dean of the House and chairman of the powerful Ways and Means Committee, once bluntly threatened to kill an entire tax bill unless a provision opposed by the cigarette manufacturers of his state was eliminated. Similarly, Chairman Eastland of the Senate Judiciary could, with the aid of several like-minded colleagues, remove the heart of Senator Kefauver's bill to stiffen Federal controls over the manufacture and pricing of drugs. Eastland's motives may have been the purest, but the relevant fact is that after Kefauver's subcommittee had taken 8,668 pages of compelling testimony, the Senator from Tennessee was not even admitted to the operating room when drastic surgery was performed on his bill. Lest anyone assume that it is only conservatives who operate with so high a hand, I hasten to add that when the late Harley Kilgore was chairman of the same committee, he flatly refused to allow it even to consider the Bricker amendment, designed to limit the treaty-making power of the President, a proposal that had wide and extremely emotional support in the Senate.

Next to control over his committee's agenda, the chairman's chief source of strength is the power he holds over his subcommittees. He appoints their chairmen, and while seniority is generally the criterion, it is by no means as rigid a rule here as it is in the naming of the committee chairman himself. A member may be ticked off to head a subcommittee as a reward for having generally gone along with his chairman, or he may be picked because he can be used to settle the fate of a particular bill. In his autobiography the refreshingly frank Wheeler leaves no doubt of the procedure so far as he was concerned:

> On other occasions, I would refer what I regarded as a bad bill to a hand-picked subcommittee, and the bill would be held there. This earned me the term "dictator," and there was some justification for it. But I knew that if certain bills ever came up for a vote in the full committee the powerful lobbies behind them would fall on the committee members and the bills would be voted out. Perhaps this was highhanded on my part, but there is no necessity for voting on every bill introduced and, rightly or wrongly, I felt in those cases I was doing what was best for my country.

If the chairman does not quite trust anybody on his committee to work his will with a particular measure, he may appoint himself to head the appropriate subcommittee. Chairman Fulbright did just that when his Banking and Currency Committee had an area redevelopment bill before it and he was thought to fear that its passage would dissuade Northern industries from moving to Arkansas. Clarence Cannon, the cranky octogenarian who heads the House Appropriations Committee, is said to have stripped one of his subcommittee chairmen of his power because he failed to slash an Administration financial request as sharply as Cannon thought right and proper. Not all committee chiefs are highhanded, of course, but it is perhaps symbolic that when one of them enters a subcommittee hearing room, the subcommittee chairman immediately rises to offer him the chair, which as a rule he graciously refuses.

A less formal power, but sometimes as devastating as any, lies in the chairman's ability to postpone meetings of his committee. He can put these off in some cases so effectively that a bill distasteful to him cannot possibly emerge before the expiration of the session. It is not quite so easy to execute this maneuver as it once was, since the convening of only seven standing committees is now left wholly to the call of the chairman. The rest meet on fixed days, weekly or biweekly. But there are ways for a skilled chairman to get around his own rules. In a meeting scheduled to run ninety minutes, for example, he may turn the floor over to chosen members for extended readings from their favorite authors. Senator Eastland managed to fill the time of the Judiciary Committee in this edifying way when the 1960 Civil Rights bill was up for consideration. According to the late Senator Hennings, members were often treated to excerpts from *Uncle Remus* and the Testaments, Old and New.

The chairman may choose to call meetings only when he

knows that a quorum cannot be obtained. With proper control over his members he can make sure that such a quorum is not available. Even though the committee may meet on its regularly appointed days, additional meetings, which are all but indispensable toward the end of a session, are subject to his call. If at that point he finds himself sour on a major proposal still before his committee, he has only to stall for a while and his problem disappears.

In such circumstances the easiest, though also the crudest, way to stall is simply to leave town. The technique was perfectly demonstrated in 1962 by Representative Wayne N. Aspinall of Colorado. In the first session of the Eighty-seventh Congress the Senate had passed a bill to preserve under Federal control a little of what is left of the American wilderness as a cultural and spiritual heritage of the nation. It was the fourth such legislative attempt, and conservationists were delighted with the emphatic 78-to-8 vote in the Senate. From unofficial canvasses of the House they anticipated an easy majority there, too, but they did not sufficiently take into account the way of a chairman with his committee or the remarkable looseness of Congressional machinery. Mr. Aspinall, chairman of the Committee on Interior and Insular Affairs, appeared to view the remaining wilderness with something of the commercial eye of the grazing and mining interests of his state, which is to say, he had little use for the bill. Three weeks before the end of the session, when the committee, overriding the chairman's feelings in the matter, voted for a revised bill, there no longer was any excuse for his failing to report it out. He therefore attempted none but quietly slipped out of Washington instead and returned to his home town of Palisade, Colorado. Congress was left to adjourn at its pleasure, without Mr. Aspinall's presence or a thought for the wilderness.

In the Representative's absence couldn't other committee members have called a committee meeting and reported the

bill to the floor? Technically, they could have. But, as another
Congressman explained, it would have been a "terrible thing
to do." They would "have to live with him afterward and work
with him again—you just don't slap down a chairman."

There are a number of reasons, besides the mellow desire to
get along with one's fellow creatures, that help explain why
members of Congress meekly accept from a committee chairman a degree of autocracy that would scandalize them in the
President of the United States. The chairman dispenses the
committee's staff jobs, a limited but still attractive bit of patronage. By his power to appoint subcommittee chairmen, already touched on, he can promote the career of a committee
colleague or seriously thwart his ambitions. And he has complete authority over the records of his committee.

In the case of subcommittee proceedings the chairman may
even dispense with records altogether. Called to the witness
stand in a contempt of Congress trial growing out of one of his
Judiciary Committee investigations, Senator Eastland contended that a subcommittee majority had authorized the closed
hearings, at which the contempt was committed, an important
legal point in the trial. His own committee counsel had previously testified that no such subcommittee meeting had been
held, and the Senator himself could not remember when or
where it had taken place, or who was there. But on his say-so
the "authorized" hearings were held. A small slice of the cross-
examination of the Senator by defense counsel Joseph L.
Rauh, Jr. suggests something of the casual way in which these
grave matters are sometimes handled:

Q. It is now your testimony that a majority of the subcommittee met. Was this called as a meeting of the subcommittee or
was this just—

A. That is the way we handled it. In fact, the full Judiciary
Committee has met off the Senate floor a number of times and
approved bills, nominations.

Q. Was there any record of this meeting?

A. I wouldn't think so. . . .

Q. Why does your committee not keep a record of these meetings if the rule requires that there be such meetings?

A. The rules never required that a record of the meetings be kept. But we kept none and have never kept a record of subcommittee meetings.

Q. You didn't mean to say before that there are no records of the subcommittee meetings, did you, Senator?

A. Well, there could be records of some of them. Certainly there can be records of some of them. I can't say that we haven't—where we take testimony, of course there is a record; but I would say this, that in most of the meetings where decisions are made or bills are reported out there is no official record.

Who is there on a committee to object to these easygoing procedures? Recalcitrant junior members are quickly squelched in the name of seniority, often with the aid of colleagues who are in substantial agreement with them. The newcomer who persistently questions the behavior of his chairman or is in general too forward may find himself isolated, without effectiveness and probably without a future on the committee. Since even the questioning of witnesses proceeds, like everything else, on the basis of seniority, he can be confined to trivia in public hearings or have his performance ruined by frequent interruptions from the chairman. He can be assigned to the least desirable subcommittees and kept from ever attaining a significant chairmanship. Writing in the *Progressive*, Sidney Lens reported a little episode that conveys the flavor of the relationship. A freshman member, ignoring tradition, called on the redoubtable Carl Vinson to explain a $50,000 item which he felt was inconsistent with past practices. "Son, I've never been consistent a day in my life," Vinson replied in the tones of a kindly parent to a presumptuous child. "If there's no objection the proposal will be considered passed."

Except in extreme cases—and these do occur—senior members are even less likely than newcomers to kick over the traces. By the very fact of their seniority they have a stake in the system and are generally convinced, moreover, that the tradition has much to be said for it.

From members of Congress outside a chairman's particular committee compliance is easily secured. For reasons already mentioned they have to rely on committee reports for guidance in matters beyond their comprehension. Second, they respect the findings of other committees and the authority of their chairmen as part of a system of reciprocal courtesy, which they may some day claim for themselves in return. And, not least, they have a lively desire to keep on good terms with men who are in a position to do them much good or considerable harm. What Senator knows when he may be going, hat in hand, to plead with the chairman of Armed Services that a defense installation be located in his district rather than in some other? What Representative knows when he will be needing the good offices of the chairman of the subcommittee on Immigration to get a constituent's relative into the country as an exception under the immigration laws—or to keep one from being deported? Praising the courage of the would-be rebel against the Establishment, Senator Douglas reminded him what he might expect to hear: "'The legislation you favor will not go through. The dam your constituents want will not be built. The river improvements your constituents want will not be made.'" And it is a naïve member who does not quickly understand that such services as these can make the difference between a brief fling on Capitol Hill and a full-blown Congressional career.

In the circumstances it is no wonder that committee chairmen have become the aristocrats of Congress, not to say the autocrats of American government. Sounded out on the prospect that he might be named Secretary of Defense, Carl Vinson, head of the House Armed Services Committee, could seriously tell a reporter, "I'd rather run the Pentagon from up here." Even the President is often no match for these princes of Capitol Hill. When President Kennedy made tax revision the most urgent item on his program, he had first to deal with Wilbur Mills, chairman of the House Ways and Means Committee, not as a trusted party lieutenant or adviser, but almost as a sovereign power.

It is routine for a President to share special White House breakfasts with subcommittee chairmen from Appropriations—an Otto Passman who must be cajoled if the President's foreign-aid program is not to be gutted entirely; a John Rooney who must be coaxed into giving the United States Information Service enough funds to perform its mission. James Reston once related how President Kennedy felt obliged to press his reluctant Vice President into doing a tiring chore for Clarence Cannon, Chairman of the House Appropriations Committee. Cannon had asked Lyndon Johnson to speak at a small Missouri college on the same day he had already agreed to speak in Texas. The Vice President's polite regrets were received with such decidedly unconcealed resentment that Mr. Kennedy, eager for the good will of the strategic chairman, prevailed on Johnson to make both talks—with great effort and the help of an Air Force jet.

In view of the power that is locked into the committees of Congress, a power that visibly affects the life of the nation, it is reasonable to consider, if only briefly, how they are put together. Concerning the making of a chairman, one can afford to be brief: it is simply a gift of time. Let us say that a Democratic Representative starts out, in a Democratic Congress, with an assignment to the Committee on Agriculture. After a term or two the Republicans take control, and since the committees generally follow the party ratio obtaining in the House as a whole, he and a few other low seniority men may be bumped off the committee entirely to make room for more Republicans. But assuming he gets through this early period of uncertainty, he is a fixture on Agriculture as long as he wants to be—and as long, of course, as his constituents keep sending him back to Congress.[2] Eventually, if he outstays his seniors, the day will come when he is the Number One veteran of the committee, and then neither ineptitude, nor political philosophy, nor even senility can stay his designation. The same is true, of course, in the Senate. Given the necessary staying power, an Eastland, after publicly urging defiance of the Supreme Court, becomes chairman of the Judiciary Committee, which passes on the appointment of Justices. Senator Capper came to a chairmanship at eighty-one, when it was said of him that he could hear no one and no one could hear him.

There have been cases where a Representative attained a committee throne in less than a decade. The twenty or so members of his own party who were ahead of him when he started out (in the Senate it would more likely be nine or ten) had vanished through death, retirement, defeat at the polls, or voluntary transfer to other committees. Others may have declined the chairmanship, and in the Senate a man is passed over if he is already chairman of another committee. But much more common is the long wait, with ambition thwarted by the longevity and political hardihood of others.

What this means in practice is that besides a good life expectancy a would-be chairman should come from a state or district where the opposition is nonexistent, or nothing to worry about. Hence the Southern grip on Congress. It is hardly

2 Once off the committee, if only for a term, he loses all seniority, and if he returns it is again as low man on the totem pole, no matter how much he knows about the subject or the ways of the committee.

coincidental that of the Senate's sixteen standing committees, nine are presently headed as follows:

FOREIGN RELATIONS, by *Fulbright* of Arkansas
FINANCE, by *Byrd* of Virginia
ARMED SERVICES, by *Russell* of Georgia
BANKING AND CURRENCY, by *Robertson* of Virginia
AGRICULTURE, by *Ellender* of Louisiana
LABOR AND PUBLIC WELFARE, by *Hill* of Alabama
JUDICIARY, by *Eastland* of Mississippi
GOVERNMENT OPERATIONS, by *McClellan* of Arkansas
POST OFFICE & CIVIL SERVICE, by *Johnston* of South Carolina
RULES AND ADMINISTRATION, by *Jordan* of North Carolina

That leaves six chairmanships for the thirty-nine states not fortunate enough to have been part of the defeated Confederacy.

The answer, one might say, especially if one were a Republican, is to elect a Republican majority and thus avoid this Southern concentration of power. But by virtue of a similar partisan maldistribution, the same Senate committees would, if the Republicans were in control, be overwhelmingly in the hands of men from rural states. In the House, fourteen of the twenty chairmanships would fall to Representatives from districts so heavily Republican as to provide no more practical opposition than Senator Russell can expect in Georgia.[3]

While seniority is the sole criterion in the making of a chairman, other elements have to go into the original committee assignments that determine a man's career in House or Senate.

[3] Admittedly, however, times are changing. Texas has for two years had a Republican Senator, and Alabama came extremely close to providing a second, a phenomenon comparable to the handwriting that spoiled Belshazzar's dinner. There is also a fair sprinkling of Republican Representatives from the states of the Old Confederacy. All of which indicates that whatever the political or social complexion of Southern Republicans, they can serve the useful purpose of ruining the built-in seniority that has for so long given the South a toe-hold on Congressional committees.

A freshman's own choice plays a part, but not a large one. Let's say that six new Senators are competing for three vacancies on the Judiciary Committee. One vacancy will be barred to all of them because a second-term Senator who has been waiting several years to get on Judiciary puts in for transfer from another committee. Since seniority among the six new applicants is equal, the assignments may be decided alphabetically, by the tossing of coins, or even by the order in which the applicants' states were admitted to the Union. But more commonly, and this is far more important, they are determined by the preferences of what Senator Clark described as The Establishment.

In each chamber of Congress, as it stands now, the two major parties have unofficial committees that draw up slates for their respective members on the all-important standing committees. Their recommendations are ratified by party caucuses and then by the full chambers as a matter of routine. For the Democrats a Steering Committee does the job in the Senate and that party's members of the Ways and Means Committee in the House. These selecting committees themselves are supposed to reflect geographic variety and ideological spread, besides naturally including the party's most influential figures in the Congress. It is the contention of critics that the first and second of these considerations are all too often lost in the shuffle.

In the Senate, the Majority and Minority leaders, their whips, and the ranking members of the major committees run the show; in the House their opposite numbers prevail. Of the fifteen members of the Democratic Steering Committee in the Senate, therefore, seven are Southerners, though their share of the chamber's total membership is at most a third. Of the same fifteen-man roster, as Clark pointed out, nine must presently be classed as conservatives—Smathers, Bible, Ellender, Hayden, Holland, Johnston, McClellan, Robertson, and Russell. A tenth, Dodd, is at least in the doubtful category, leaving only Mansfield, Humphrey, Douglas, Williams, and Clark to represent the political position advanced by the party platform and upheld by its successful nominee for the Presidency.

On the House side, since the Democrats of the Ways and Means Committee double in brass as their party's committee on committees, the self-perpetuation of power is simple and inevitable. A committee headed during the past decade by Robert L. Doughton (N.C.), Jere Cooper (Tenn.), and Wilbur Mills (Ark.) could hardly have been expected to change either ways or means in the House of Representatives.

Besides making awards for seniority, these committees on committees do employ other criteria. The geographical composition of the standing committees is one consideration, the interest, livelihood and experience of the applying member is another, and influential support for his choice can be a third. Former Representative Jerry Voorhis observed in his *Confessions of A Congressman* that the House Agriculture Committee represented the five basic commodities. "The main interests of the overwhelming majority of the committee were—and still are—summed up in 'cotton, tobacco, wheat, corn, and hogs.'" Which is probably as close as we can come to representation by guilds.

But beyond any of these considerations is the degree to which the applicant for a committee post has proved, or at least pledged, his cooperation with the powers that be. Senators Clark, Douglas, and Proxmire charged, early in the life of the Eighty-eighth Congress, that Senators who fought to modify the institution of the filibuster were punished in the awarding of committee plums. They could not prove it, but they did make a case. Eight Senators who stood with the Establishment, as it were, in opposition to any change in the rules, had, as it happened, put in requests for new committee assignments. Seven were accommodated, six getting their first choice. On the

other hand, of fourteen Senators who struck a blow against the
filibuster and who likewise had asked for new assignments,
only five were accommodated. Of these, moreover, only one
got the committee of his choice—and he was the Majority
Leader, whose claim could hardly be denied.[4]

What is more, some of these antifilibuster men were bypassed in favor of men with less seniority or no seniority at all.
Senator Hart of Michigan and Senator Moss of Utah, for example, both applied for assignment to the Armed Services
Committee. Both would be up for re-election the following
year and would need all the prestige possible to win. But both
favored curtailing the Senate's custom of limitless debate, and
when committee posts were passed around, the vacancy on
Armed Services went instead to Daniel Inouye, the freshman
Senator from Hawaii. He had voted against changing the debate rule even though his state had been kept out of the
Union for years by just such parliamentary devices.

Drastic defection from the leadership is naturally treated
more drastically. Back in 1925, thirteen Republican members
from Wisconsin were stripped of their seniority and demoted
to the bottom rungs of lowly committees for having the year
before supported the Third Party campaign of Senator La Follette against Calvin Coolidge. "In Congress they asked to be

---

[4] In the midst of the Clark assault, Senator Russell of Georgia
took the floor to defend the privileged position of the majority
and minority leaders in the choice of committee assignments:
". . . heaven knows, they undergo enough torture. I have heard
questions asked them for thirty years. Senators come up to them
and say, 'What time are we going to vote? What time are we
going to vote?' Of course, neither the majority leader nor the
minority leader knows any more about the time the Senate is going
to vote than does the Senator asking the question, but he is supposed to have some pleasant and reasonable answer." Renouncing
all ambition for leadership himself, Russell concluded: "Heaven
forbid. Life is short enough without undertaking to answer 2,000
questions a day when I would not have the remotest idea what the
answers might be."

restored to full membership on the councils of the party which they had done their best to destroy," said Speaker Nicholas Longworth. "They wanted high positions in the key committees. We said no, that they had to start over if they wanted to be Republicans." Similarly, Wayne Morse in 1953 was deprived of his prized posts on the Armed Services and Labor Committees for having abandoned the Republican Party to support Adlai Stevenson. As an "Independent," he found neither party interested in his committee standing and had to join the Democratic Party officially before being restored to his old position.

On the face of it, neither of these actions would seem to be unreasonable. Why should a party bypass its own members in favor of an outsider, if not an outright opponent? In fact *party* responsibility would be highly desirable in a body where responsibility is now so fragmented. And a party can hardly be held to account if it is denied the minimal right to withhold favor from followers who engage in full-scale rebellion. The logic would, I think, be unimpeachable were it not for the fact that far greater party disloyalty by States' Rights Democrats is so accepted that it has virtually become a Congressional way of life. La Follette and his followers went off the reservation once, but there are Democrats in Congress who vote with their own party majority no more than a third of the time, and they are *chairmen of committees*. There are Southern Democrats who for years have not supported their party's candidate for President and who openly disavow their party's platform, and yet, as Democrats, they remain movers and shakers in the Congress. The States' Rights ticket in 1948 actually defeated Harry Truman in four states, costing him thirty-nine electoral votes. Eight Democratic Senators and thirty Representatives actively campaigned against him, and in Alabama the Dixiecrats went so far as to bar the Democratic ticket from the ballot. Yet no disciplinary action whatever was taken by the loyalist wing of the Democratic Party in Congress. The argument was that the revolt was simply too massive. Had discipline been attempted, it was believed, the States Righters, with nothing more to lose, would have joined forces with the Republicans. The Senate would then have been delivered over to the opposition and the Democratic majority in the House would have been reduced to a scant seventeen.

The price might still have been reasonable, but to have paid it would have shaken American political life to the roots, possibly destroyed the Democratic Party, and at least pointed the way to an ultimate realignment of parties along ideological lines. Since neither the Truman Administration nor the Northern Democrats in Congress were at the time ready for anything nearly so drastic, all was forgiven, though probably not forgotten. A two-headed donkey continued to function on Capitol Hill, with the rebel head retaining the louder voice in The Establishment.

It is this fact, presumably, rather than the mere existence of an Establishment, that provokes the ire of the Clarks and the Douglases. For, except in the visions of anarchists, political organisms do not operate, after all, by spontaneous action; somewhere in them there must reside an element of conscious political power. The problem is not to eliminate, or even necessarily to weaken, an Establishment as such within the Congress, but only to make it more responsible to the electorate than it is at present. That means to make it more dependent on a current majority *party* which must regularly account to the voters. Unfortunately for the Democrats, and for the country, they cannot be regarded as that kind of party as long as they are *two* parties, one of which is willing to be responsible to the electorate only if it can hand-pick the voters.

Having scanned the elements of the committee system and touched on Senator Clark's Establishment, we should be somewhat prepared now to understand the impact of the system, with all its oddities, on the issue of our particular interest.

4

Here Lie the School Bills

The Dilatory Seventy-ninth

In January, 1945, the Seventy-ninth Congress met in an expectant and forward-looking mood. Hitler's Thousand-Year Reich was cracking some 988 years ahead of schedule, the defeat of Japan was only a question of time, and the country's thoughts were turning toward those long-awaited improvements that would adorn the bright and peaceful years ahead. Not least among these advances, as reflected in the minds of Congressmen, was to be the salvation of the nation's school system from hard-pressed mediocrity through regular and substantial injections of Federal money.

The idea was far from new. The House of Representatives had passed just such a bill as long ago as Grant's Administration, but the Senate had said no. Then, to restore the balance, Senator Blair of New Hampshire had three times in the 1880s

74

driven similar bills through the Senate, only to find that the House had changed its mind and was no longer interested. Under President Hoover and in the early days of the Roosevelt Administration official commissions of distinguished and expert citizens had made studies—one of them ran to thirteen volumes —and brought in reports proving that state resources were inadequate to the fast-growing educational needs of the country.

But now the experience of war had again given fresh impetus to the demand. Even in World War 1 a shocking proportion of young American males had been found as useless for modern battle as a mob of Egyptian *fellahin,* being wholly innocent of the power to read, write, or count beyond the number of toes on their feet. Those who thought about such matters had been concerned enough then; but since 1918, warfare (an ironic device to measure educational need) had become overwhelmingly technical and was getting more so every month. Yet illiteracy was still so intensive that of the five million men rejected for service in World War II, it is reliably estimated that some two million might have been assets but for the lack of a fourth-grade education.

Add to this jolting fact the staggering need for new school buildings, a backlog built up and waiting through four years of war, plus the drastic shortage of teachers willing to work at long outmoded rates of pay, and by 1945 the receptiveness of Congress to proposals for financial aid was almost inevitable. At long last, it seemed, the time had come.

Almost immediately, identical bills, inspired and promoted by the National Education Association, were introduced under impeccable sponsorship—in the House by Ramspeck of Georgia, in the Senate by Hill of Alabama and Thomas of Utah, all members of their respective Committees on Education and all members of the majority Democratic Party. The measures would have given the states $200 million as an emergency war fund for immediate spending on their elementary and secondary public schools, and $100 million annually thereafter. The emergency appropriation was to have been divided according to population; the annual grant, according to a formula that took into account both school-age population and income.

With admirable dispatch the Senate Committee on Education and Labor, chaired by James E. Murray of Montana, opened hearings on January 29, and six days later it had sympathetically listened to seventy-one witnesses, whose overwhelmingly favorable testimony filled a 430-page volume. Dr. John K. Norton, of Teachers College, Columbia University, set the tone and to a considerable degree fixed the pattern of argument for proponents of Federal aid for many a hearing to come: (1) The "educational slums" of the country were a "repudiation of one of the most sacred ideals of American life, the ideal of equal opportunity." (2) The extent of illiteracy, a direct result of insufficient State funds for education, had become a threat to the national defense. (3) Adequate education was a sound, long-term national investment—the reasonably educated paid more taxes than the unschooled and were much less of a financial drain on society.

The Committee was impressed. Senator Ellender of Louisiana, besides putting in a good word for the educated soldiers of Russia, could hardly restrain his praise: "Doctor, you made a most excellent witness. I wish every member of Congress had heard your testimony."

Opposition was minimal, and for the most part none too well received. Major General Amos A. Fries was concerned about the dangers of "centralized Federal control," but his prestige as Director of the Southern-Western Region of the Friends of the Public Schools of America was deflated by Senator Fulbright's questioning: "If you are a friend of the public schools, how do you help? Is this the only program that you indulge in; that is, fighting the Federal appropriations?" To which the General was forced to reply that it was not, his organization also published an eight-page monthly bulletin for "maybe 1,000 members, maybe more or maybe less." Merwin K. Hart's National Economic Council, in temper a forerunner of the John Birch Society, was duly recorded in opposition, and so was something called the "Wheel of Progress," whose President-General, Mrs. Margaret Hopkins Worrell, did not think it was money that the schools needed. "Let us get back to base, and drop this 'progressive education' which is no education at all," she urged. "Ground the children in the fundamentals and there will be no such illiteracy as is now complained of."

A representative from the United States Chamber of Commerce refrained from taking any position on the bill, contenting himself and the Committee with figures showing an undeniable connection between education and the production of income. Even more striking, in view of later events, the NAACP was unequivocally for the bill in spite of the fact that it would add evenhandedly to the amounts spent on white and colored children, ignoring an existing discrepancy that in some states ran as high as six to one. Answering Senator Aiken's unbelieving query on this point, the Association's Leslie S. Perry was a model of forbearance:

> *Senator Aiken:* As I understand it you would rather see the Southern States receive $7 more for the education of each Negro child, even though the white children were to get the same amount, than to see no increase whatsoever?
>
> *Mr. Perry:* Let me say here that we are not particularly concerned about the ceiling on white education, for example. If, in a public school, there is $50 appropriated for Negroes and $50 appropriated for whites, and through voluntary donations, for example, they want to raise the white standard to $100 per child, we wouldn't be concerned about that. We are simply interested in certain minimum standards for Negroes.

The only cloud on the horizon of the bill's proponents was the brief testimony of Monsignor Frederick G. Hochwalt, speaking for the National Catholic Welfare Conference. It did not seem to be a large cloud. Monsignor Hochwalt left no doubt of the Church's attitude about a bill that was not "equitable to all children in the area of need without regard to color, origin, or creed," but his statement had a resigned and unemotional tone that gave no indication of what was about to happen.

Monsignor Hochwalt's testimony was given on February 1, and after two more sessions the committee recessed on the 8th, subject to the call of the chairman. One month later Senator Aiken, whose state of Vermont had an unusually high percentage of private schools, and Senator Mead of New York introduced a brand-new bill, one that would allow private and denominational as well as public schools to benefit from the Federal largesse. Inspiration for the move came, not from the National Catholic Welfare Council, but from the American Federation of Labor, attracted in part by the higher appropriation and the greater emphasis on teachers' pay. Its affiliated American Federation of Teachers would now contend openly with the rival National Education Association for Congressional favor.

Hearings were resumed on April 11, and they were considerably more heated than the earlier set. For the National Catholic Welfare Council, the Reverend William E. McManus regretted that his organization had been forced to oppose Federal aid bills in the past because they favored only public schools, rejoiced that he could now support "a bill recognizing a principle of justice," and wound up with a warning that "we are absolutely opposed to any change in this bill which would exclude nonpublic schools" from its benefits. A representative of the Religious Liberty Association countered with a document containing a plea by a former Governor of Virginia headed, "To the Dikes! To the Dikes! O Baptists!" And Ben-

jamin C. Marsh, for many years spokesman for the Peoples
Lobby, Inc., feverishly asked whether the AFL and the CIO
had become "stooges of the Vatican." The Teachers Union, a
CIO affiliate, denied that it favored the Mead-Aiken bill at
all and clucked disapprovingly over the position taken by its
opposite number in the AFL. From that union, the American
Federation of Teachers, came a bewildering conflict of testimony. Selma Borchardt, its Vice President and Washington
spokesman, was eloquently in favor of the provision to include
private and parochial schools. But Dr. Floyd W. Reeves,
chairman of the Federation's Commission of Educational Re-
construction, whom Miss Borchardt presented with a flourish
as the organization's expert technician, seemed taken aback
by the private school clause and repudiated it on the spot. A
majority of his own Commission, he said, was opposed to such
aid.

Eleven more days were consumed in these hearings, with
eighty witnesses heard in addition to the seventy-one who had
already appeared. And while they proceeded, under the be-
nevolent eye of the chairman, a companion bill introduced in
The House by Representative Ramspeck started through the
less friendly course laid out by the chamber's Committee
on Education. The Ramspeck bill, which was the same as the
Senate's Hill-Thomas bill, was quickly followed by one introduced by Representative Lesinski of Michigan, which would
have allowed private and parochial schools in under the um-
brella, paralleling the Mead-Aiken bill in the Senate. But
where the Senate committee was headed by a Catholic and
was in any case more open to compromise, the chairman
of the House committee was Graham Barden of North Carolina, a Southern Presbyterian with strong feelings on the subject. They were not of the sort that embraced aid to parochial
schools in any way, shape, or form, and his course therefore

was simple. As chairman he simply saw to it that House hearings were confined to bills for aid to public schools only.[1] The Committees of both Houses completed hearings late in the spring of 1945, but further action was postponed by the general confusion into which the Congressional agenda was thrown by the sudden death of President Roosevelt and, soon after, the defeat of Germany.

Not until the end of October did the Senate Committee return to the problem of reconciling its two bills. To Chairman Murray it then seemed that the best way to achieve this purpose was to appoint a new subcommittee, which he did, letting it wrestle with a fresh draft. Headed by Hill of Alabama, the subcommittee was a nicely balanced group, consisting of Democrats Ellender of Louisiana, Chavez of New Mexico, and Tunnell of Delaware, Republicans Taft of Ohio and Aiken of Vermont; and La Follette of Wisconsin, who was then listed as a Progressive. In spite of Aiken's presence, there was little chance that this group would recommend including aid to parochial schools, and it did not. Its revised bill would have authorized a permanent system of Federal grants rising to $250 million in the third year to all but the richest states—but to be used for public schools only. The subcommittee had been in no hurry, however, and neither was the full committee, with the result that it was the following June 13 before the amended version was reported to the Senate itself.

In the meantime, however, the Ramspeck bill had come a cropper in the House. Redrafted by its original sponsor, it had been reintroduced on December 7, 1945, promptly referred

[1] Following the reorganization of Congress in 1946, the Labor and Education Committees were merged. Rep. Lesinski, with more seniority, became the chairman, and was only succeeded by Barden again in 1951. Relations between the two men, not good at best, were to have a bearing on the fate of school bills for a decade.

back to the Committee on Education, and killed by it on December 12, which shows how fast Congress can move when the purpose is negative. What had happened was that the full Committee took a quick vote on whether to report the bill out, and the result was 10 to 9 against. Absent were two Democrats, whose votes might well have made the difference. Why did Chairman Barden, who was nominally for the bill, not wait for a more propitious moment, instead of rushing the decision in five days? It was the beginning of a long period in which, as a Committee member years later confided, the suspicion persisted that the gentleman from North Carolina "only pretended to favor the legislation," while alert for any and every opportunity to do it in.

When the Senate Committee finally got around to making its report in June of 1946, its backers quickly conceded that there was too little time left in the session both to get it passed in the Senate and to get it considered as a fresh bill in a House Committee that had in effect already voted it down. Accordingly, on August 1, Senator Hill rose to express his "profound regret" that necessary postwar legislation allowed too little time to bring the Federal aid bill to the floor for debate.

> This regret is all the more pronounced in view of the strong position taken on the bill by the Committee on Education and Labor and in view of my belief, with which others concur, that the bill as reported by the committee has the support of a substantial majority of the Members of the United States Senate. . . . When the new Congress convenes, it seems to me its first days should be distinguished by enactment of legislation as embodied in Senate bill 181. There is no reason for delay with further hearings. We have the facts. We know the need. We must have action.

More remarkable was the hearty concurrence of Senator Robert A. Taft, a major power in the Senate and a fresh convert to the cause of Federal aid to the schools. In spite of his

long-standing conviction that "education is a state and local
responsibility," Taft told the Senate: "the Federal Government
does have a responsibility to see that every child in the United
States has at least a minimum education in order that each
child may have the opportunity which lies at the very base
of the whole system of our Republic." And, like Hill, he finished with an eye on the Congress to follow: ". . . when the
Senate reconvenes, and comes to consider the matter, it will
find that the bill prescribes a sound policy of Federal aid to
education and avoids the dangers relative to such a system."

The Education Committees of the Seventy-ninth Congress
had fumbled close to the goal, but "Mr. Republican," as Taft
was already being called, had been won over, and passage by
the 80th Congress looked almost assured.

Halfway in the Eightieth

Two developments in 1946, one long-range in its implications
and one immediate, were to have a decided effect on the
future of Federal aid to the schools. In that year Congress
passed the La Follette-Monroney Legislative Reorganization
Act, one of its rare and widely spaced recognitions that its
own functioning was not as smooth as it might be. And in the
same year the Republicans won the Congressional elections.

Among the reforms Congress imposed on itself by the La
Follette-Monroney Act was the eliminating of surplus committees and the combining of others. The move was admirable
and indeed overdue—the House had forty-five committees at
the time and the Senate thirty-three—but the particular combining of the Labor and Education committees in the House
was neither logical nor fortunate. In its very nature legislation
affecting trade unions arouses strong emotion, and the continuing clash between prolabor and antilabor members has
proved less than ideal for establishing that consensus, that

climate of accommodation, which is the basic function of a committee. In this connection it was particularly unfortunate that the newly merged committee should have had for its baptismal engagement the stormy Taft-Hartley Act. In their excellent study on "National Politics and Federal Aid to Education," Frank J. Munger and Richard F. Fenno, Jr. underscore the effect of the merger:

> Also, educational controversy has been infected with the by-products of labor controversy. Doubtless, internal conflict would be harsh enough in a single education committee, but the tradition of charge and counter-charge accompanying labor-management legislation has certainly not made it any easier for the building of consensus among the same people in another area. There is, of course, an affinity of philosophy between the supporters of organized labor and the supporters of Federal aid to education. The record of the AFL-CIO on behalf of Federal aid is proof enough. Nonetheless, the Democratic membership of the Committee has been chosen in such a way as to maximize unity on labor matters and with strictly secondary concern for unity on Federal aid.

The incoherence of the new committee on matters educational was to show itself strongly over the years in the form of pulling and hauling in executive session and simple evasion in public, but for immediate purposes the effect of the Republican victory at the polls was more obvious. By sheer seniority —no other reason could possibly have been adduced—the chairmanship of the merged committee fell to Representative Fred Hartley of New Jersey, the Republican who could claim the longest, though hardly most consistent, service, his absentee record in the House having bordered on the notorious. Representative Mary Norton, who had served as chairman of the separate Labor Committee, was so incensed at Hartley's elevation that she went to the astonishing length of resigning from the committee altogether, sacrificing her long-acquired seniority rather than serve under a man who, she said, had attended only six meetings of his former committee in ten years.

The 1946 election gave the chairmanship of the corresponding Senate Committee to Robert A. Taft, but the effect was far different. As conservative as Hartley in labor matters, Taft was far more open-minded on the general question of the Federal government's role in social matters. If the two chairmen agreed that the role should be limited to absolute essentials, they differed sharply on what was essential. "In matters affecting the necessities of life," went the Taft view, "—and I should like to confine it so far as possible to the necessities of life, namely to relief, to education, to health, and to housing—I do not believe the Federal government can say it has no interest, and say to the people, 'Go your way and do the best you can'." Taft's influence, not only as chairman—that would last only two years—but as the very voice of responsible conservatism, was decisive in the Senate committee and possibly in the Senate itself.

In spite of Senator Hill's hopeful rhetoric at the close of the Seventy-ninth, its successor Congress did not make Federal aid to the schools its first order of business or, indeed, get around to it at all for some three months. And when it did, the Senate Committee proceeded to hold hearings all over again, although Hill had rightly said that all the facts were in. Whether any minds were changed by another 600 pages of testimony is highly doubtful, but since four freshly drawn bills were up for consideration now, it was thought best to do so. Two would have appropriated funds to be used solely to boost teachers' salaries; one was a revision of the Aiken bill, including private schools in whatever benefits were to be conferred; and one (S. 472) was a modification of the Hill-Thomas bill of the earlier Congress, now blessed by Taft. Intended to equalize educational opportunity in the various states, the bill offered Federal help only where state and local funds were shown to

be inadequate to provide a minimum program. And it sought
to get around the growing religious problem by providing that
a recipient State could give some of the money to nonpublic
schools, but only for those purposes for which it was already
expending public funds, such as bus transportation and textbooks.

For the most part the same witnesses showed up and said
much the same things they had said before. Dr. Norton was
on hand again, in support of S. 472, and likewise Mr. Perry,
for the NAACP, who was as conciliatory as ever: "I want to
reiterate that we do not regard this legislation as a means of
eliminating segregation in the South." Similarly in favor was
the South Carolina Education Association, which introduced
into the record, by way of support, the inaugural remarks of
that State's new governor, the Honorable Strom Thurmond,
who was rarely thereafter in agreement with the NAACP.
"It is illogical to oppose Federal aid for education," said that
champion of States' rights, "and at the same time advocate
Federal aid for road construction and other purposes."

On the proposed compromise concerning parochial schools,
opinion varied but was generally mild. The NEA thought the
new provision "consistent with the organic laws, the traditions,
and the legal precedents of our republic. . . ." Father
McManus declared it a reasonable approach but wanted it
liberalized to allow for states that forbade all aid to sectarian
schools. The League of Women Voters felt that the provision
deviated some from the principle of public funds for public
purposes but did not regard "this defect as serious enough
to prevent our general approval of the bill." Only Senator
Donnell, a member of the subcommittee and a determined
foe of "expediency" in this matter, made no attempt to hide
his disappointment:

> As I read this bill, the money can be used for any purpose and
> I certainly most strongly disagree with you that that is a mere,

slight deviation and I want to emphasize again that even if it were only a slight deviation, personally I am opposed to it one hundred percent because I think that the matter of slight deviations leads inevitably . . . to a great departure.

The Senator could draw comfort only from Ben Marsh, of the Peoples Lobby, who was on hand again to oppose all such machinations: "I trust that you will report this bill out purged of this un-American provision. . . ."

Probably nothing in the eleven days of hearings was more effective than the testimony of two country schoolteachers. From Hampden, Maine, a teacher-principal came to tell the subcommittee what she did for the munificent $1,260 a year that she was paid:

Besides my teaching duties I am responsible for part of the janitor work. Besides tending the furnace, cleaning of our room, washing windows, care of our old-fashioned dry toilets, scrubbing the drinking fountain, displaying the flag, and looking after snow . . . I am personally responsible for fire drills, schoolboy patrol, and part of the playground duty.

And from Mrs. Nannie Rucker the Senators learned a little about finances in a rural Negro school in Rutherford County, Tennessee:

My school has enrolled this year forty-one students, and my average daily attendance is usually around thirty students, grades one through eight. . . . I am thirty-four years of age and have taught fourteen years and have completed three and a half years of college work. . . . My present total salary is $133 per month for only eight months in the year. However, after taxes and retirement payments are deducted, my net monthly salary is $110.95 or $886 per year.

On July 3, 1947, S. 472 was favorably reported out by the full Senate Committee, but by then it was too late in the session to bring it to the floor and it had to go over to the second session of the Congress. It was March 23, 1948, before it was at last called up and after a week's debate it was passed by the Senate by the thumping vote of 58 to 22. Fewer than half of the 22 who voted against the bill were antagonized by the marginal help provided for nonpublic schools; the others were conservatives of a variety too extreme to feel comfortable about Federal aid for anything more than the postal service. Significantly, a proposed amendment to bar all forms of aid to parochial schools lost by the emphatic margin of 80 to 5, an indication of how little feeling the issue was generating at that time. Senator McMahon's amendment to give the parochial schools even more, however, was also beaten back, 66 to 14.

The Senate had barely completed hearings the previous Spring when the House Education and Labor Committee called its own hearings, and back trooped most of the same witnesses with mostly the same testimony. One might well ask why the two committees could not have done the job jointly, thus saving the witnesses much wear and tear, not to mention the wear and tear on future students of the subject and the cost to taxpayers in duplicated expenditures for witnesses' travel, printing, paper, and the like. But joint hearings in Congress are reserved only for rare and special matters. If they were resorted to as a rule, too many painful questions would arise. Which House would get the combined committee chairmanship? What would become of protocol and prerogative? With the committee doubled in size, when would the members of low seniority ever get a turn to question a witness? And most important, how could committees of drastically different composition, each barely used to the give and take of its own members, be quickly reconciled to each other's ways, rules, and political perspectives?

The last of these points would, in this case, have presented the most obvious difficulty. No fewer than thirteen bills calling for some sort of Federal aid to the schools had been introduced in the House, and Mr. Hartley, the Republican chairman of the full committee, was hostile to all of them. The ranking Democrat, Mr. Lesinski, was committed to including the parochial schools in any aid bill, but he was not active in the matter, being more interested, in any case, in the labor aspects of this committee's work. Ranking just below him, Mr. Barden was even more insistent that whatever aid was to be forthcoming must *not* include parochial schools, and he was cool on the whole issue. No attempt was made to combine the various bills or to crystallize support around any one of them. Openly antagonistic, Hartley threw the ball to a subcommittee, which for seventeen days listened to uncoordinated, and often irrelevant, testimony on the general subject.

The tone of the questioning was very different from that of the Senate committee. Dr. Norton, patiently going through his paces once again, was frequently brought up sharp by the sarcasm of Rep. Gwinn of New York, who at one point expressed surprise that Norton had been appearing before Congress for a quarter of a century in pursuit of some sort of help for the public schools.

Dr. Norton: It is a tragedy, isn't it?

Rep. Gwinn: I wonder if it is.

Norton: I think so. There has been a whole generation of children, half the children of the United States, denied a decent educational opportunity. That, to me, is one of the blackest marks against the American system.

Rep. Gwinn: You were saying about the same thing twenty-five years ago that you are saying now, namely, that the American way of life was so imperiled if the Federal government didn't come to the aid of these backward States, these poor States, from which we get the money, that we would be sunk.

Another witness, who had, after all, come voluntarily to give the subcommittee the benefit of her thoughts in the matter, was taken aback when Mr. Gwinn, with all the majesty of Congress behind him, leaned over the table to mutter: "I know you are trying to salve your conscience on that point." Rep. Schwabe of Missouri could be even ruder and less relevant than Gwinn, as indicated by the following interruption in the testimony of Kermit Eby of the CIO, who had just been discussing the need of education in the strengthening of the country:

> *Rep Schwabe:* I was just wondering, as you were talking, about building stronger Americans, why you should advocate more education on the part of individual citizens when the CIO has been for industry-wide bargaining to relieve the individual of the necessity for shifting for himself. . . .

The hearings dragged on in this desultory and uncoordinated way, marked by acrimonious exchanges and without any effort to find a common ground. Since the Senate had voted so overwhelmingly for a general aid-to-education bill, there must be at least the presumption that a majority of the House might likewise have favored the measure. But because its Committee on Education and Labor was composed as it was, and because it was under no compulsion to get down to cases, this possible majority had no chance to exercise its prerogative. Had it been given even an adverse report, it would have had that chance, but instead, Mr. Hartley's committee found a pigeonhole large enough to accommodate all thirteen bills.

Twenty national organizations bombarded Speaker Martin with pleas to push the measure. But while he was generally for it, the Speaker said, he thought foreign aid and national defense should be considered first, though President Truman assured him these other needs presented "no valid reason for delaying Federal aid to education," which would be "a major contribution to the vitality of American democracy . . ." Ignoring these nudges, as well as a telegram signed by eighty prominent educators and publishers, the House Committee declined to be pushed and that was the end of the matter as far as the Eightieth Congress was concerned. Another month of hearings, another thousand printed pages of testimony, another week's debate in the Senate, all went down the drain— not because a bill was defeated, fairly and on deliberation, but because a lackadaisical committee just didn't feel up to either working out a compromise or passing a bill along.

Dead End in the Eighty-first

The dismal fate of its 1947 efforts notwithstanding, the Senate again started off with high hopes two years later. Dispensing for once with hearings in a matter on which it had already made up its mind, the Senate Committee on Labor and Public Welfare, on March 18th *unanimously* reported out a bill similar to S. 472. It was a skillful compromise, invoking the equalization principle but providing some flat grants; authorizing expenditures for teachers' salaries and current operating costs, but not for construction; and allowing states that already permitted public money to be spent on nonpublic schools for transportation and textbooks to use their Federal grants for the same purposes. Senator Hill launched the floor debate on April 29, 1949, with an eloquent reminder that the crisis had deepened since a *New York Times* survey three years before had found that although the schools of America had suffered no air raids, neglect of education was wrecking them as surely as though they had been blasted by bombers. After five days of intermittent debate, the bill was passed, 58 to 15, with 17 of the 23 nonvoters announced in its favor. Even Senator Donnell went along, although the Senate again beat back his amendment to restrict aid to public schools only—this time by a vote of 71 to 3.

It must be observed at this point, however, that the much talked of "courtesy" on Capitol Hill is not carried to such extremes that a bill endorsed by 78 percent of the Senate is automatically deemed worthy of even being offered for the consideration of the House. In this case, Rep. Barden, chairman of the special subcommittee appointed by Lesinski, declared himself a convert to the cause, but so cranky was his conditional and fearful approach and so domineering his conduct of the hearings, that proponents would have preferred his outright opposition.

With Committee Chairman Lesinski otherwise occupied, Barden from the first adopted a stance toward his subcommittee that suggested a top sergeant running company headquarters in the absence of an officer and reveling in the opportunity. No sooner had the Senate's bill been referred to his group, early in May, than he announced simply that "There are some features in the Senate bill so objectionable to me that I could not find myself going over to it. I am not going to accept it; that's all." Instead he substituted his own bill (H. R. 4643), which would have restricted Federal funds to public schools only and also eliminated the Senate's requirement of periodic reports by the states to the Federal Commissioner of Education.

The hearings, which brought all the familiar voices back to Capitol Hill, ran eleven days and amounted to nearly a thousand printed pages of sparring between Barden and those among the forty-eight witnesses who did not see eye to eye with him. There was to be no hint of Federal control, such as the report requirement, because, Barden explained, that sort of thing was acceptable only in degenerate urban centers, where cowed citizens "get in the habit of going where the cops tell them to go and where the guard says they cannot go they do not go. . . ." Country folks in contrast, "are still Americans and believe that this question of freedom and rights and so forth is an active question right now, and you must bear that in mind."

Again and again the chairman seemed to be sounding a note of alarm even about his own bill. Here he is in typical colloquy with the Commissioner of Education, Earl J. McGrath:

> *Barden:* Then if you were sitting in my place, you would be pretty cautious, would you not, in proceeding?
>
> *McGrath:* Yes, I see the dangers that you see. I do.
>
> *Barden:* Do they scare you as bad as they do me?
>
> *McGrath:* I do not believe so.

Witnesses who objected to the exclusion of private and parochial schools from even the auxiliary benefits to be conferred were given short shrift. One labor spokesman received the lordly advice: "I am frank to state to you that your idea will not pass." Another witness was told: "One ear is deaf and the other is partly closed when you talk to me." And when President Eklund of the American Federation of Teachers criticized the chairman's particular bill, his good faith as a proponent of *any* Federal aid to the schools was laid open to question.

> *Barden:* I could not help interrupting the gentleman because he has consumed about twenty-five minutes here and has not said one single good word here for the legislation pending before the committee, and yet you represent the teachers of the United States, you say.
>
> *Eklund:* Now, wait a minute—
>
> *Barden:* If there is anything good you can say about a bill, or if there is any contribution you can make toward helping a piece of legislation through, I think your teachers would appreciate it.

Regardless of the merits of the parochial school question, Barden's heavy-handedness quickly succeeded in creating an atmosphere in which no proposed school legislation could be expected to pass. The first public reaction, hardly less ponderous than Barden's own approach, was Francis Cardinal Spellman's comment at Fordham University, identifying Barden as a "new apostle of bigotry" and calling for a share of Federal aid for parochial schools in the name of "freedom of religion and freedom of education." By way of answer, Methodist Bishop G. Bromley Oxnam accused the Cardinal of "bearing false witness" against Mr. Barden, and if that exchange was not enough to sour the climate for any bill, this end was achieved shortly after, when the Cardinal denounced three newspaper columns by Eleanor Roosevelt, all in opposition to Federal aid to parochial schools, as an "anti-Catholic campaign" and as "documents of discrimination unworthy of an American mother."

Eventually the Spellman-Roosevelt argument was smoothed over—the Cardinal said he wanted no general public support of religious schools but only "auxiliary services" and Mrs. Roosevelt called his statement "clarifying and fair"—but not before countless individuals and newspapers had been drawn into the fray and a great deal of bitterness engendered. In the end Bishop Oxnam charged the Catholic hierarchy with "killing the bills that might have brought Federal aid to our public school system" and of trying to "get its hands into the public treasury."

More to the point, John Lesinski, chairman of the full House Education and Labor Committee, was enraged on receiving the Barden bill from his subcommittee. It was an "anti-Catholic" bill, he said, filled with "bigotry and racial prejudice." What was more, the man he had appointed to head that subcommittee, Lesinski charged, "drew it up that way purposely because he didn't want any aid to education and wanted to

kill it." Barden said he was "utterly astounded." As far as the
bill itself was concerned, the cry of bigotry was unwarranted.
The most that could be said was that, unlike the Senate bill,
Barden's would not even have allowed Federal funds to be
spent on transportation or textbooks for non-public schools
in states that already permitted such expenditure of public
money. As for Barden's intentions, however, it must at least
be allowed that he had taken a curious attitude toward his
bill, that he had never been much in favor of Federal aid to
the schools before and that he was to show still less fervor in
the future.

In any case, Lesinski swore that the Barden bill would
never be reported out of his committee, and he had the
arbitrary powers with which all chairman are endowed. In
fact, it was ignored. Instead, the full committee took up the
neglected Senate bill once more, but feeling was so high by
then that, on an unrecorded vote, it was defeated 11 to 14.
A motion to put the whole question off to the following year
was then made by a second-term Representative named John
F. Kennedy, and it lost, too, by one vote. Nevertheless, the
thin majority against postponing was unable to agree on a fresh
approach, and the bill lay over until the next session, even
without benefit of a motion.

Responding to a plea by President Truman, the committee
met in executive session in February, 1950, and reconsidered
S. 246, but even within the committee the bill was attacked
from two sides. Referring to the Spellman-Roosevelt exchange,
Barden had remarked that the controversy made members
very cautious. "Before it came up, it would have passed the
House three to one," he remarked. "Now nobody knows."
Barden and his faction were no more satisfied than before
with the loophole through which parochial schools would have
received some funds for transportation and books; and some
of the Catholic members, including Chairman Lesinski him-

self, did not seem to think that the parochial schools would do well enough under the bill. Others were evidently disturbed by the equalization principle. Coming from relatively poor districts of relatively rich states, they could not see their constituents happily giving out of their taxes considerably more than they would receive under the program.

Attempting to patch up the Senate bill, Lesinski set aside a full month, from February 6, for closed committee sessions, and while the debate was therefore off the record, some of its fruitless proceedings have since leaked out. Barden immediately reintroduced his flat ban on aid to nonpublic schools. Rep. Kearns, the ranking Republican on the subcommittee and a former school superintendent, was upset by a Federal Security Administration pamphlet on sex education, entitled "Your Child from 6 to 12," and demanded that President Truman promise that the agency would keep its hands off the schools if the bill was passed. No sooner did that tempest subside than Barden, choosing the moment with diabolical skill, made a speech in New York blaming the Catholic Church for having fatally injected the religious issue. To which Cardinal Spellman responded with the heated prophecy that "Tomorrow they will try to keep us out of the public libraries, the public gardens, and perhaps off the sidewalks," and once more the fate of the bill was sealed. Proposed amendments to bar funds for private schools were again defeated, but so was Rep. Kennedy's to allow help for all school bus systems.

In the end the Committee refused, by a vote of 13 to 12, even to report the Senate bill out. Agreeing for once, but only because they could all be in the negative, were Chairman Lesinski and ranking minority member McConnell; Subcommittee Chairman Barden and Mr. Kearns; and, not least, those two young members and men of destiny, Representatives Kennedy and Nixon.

So it was that in the six years that followed the war, when

the need was most acute, at least thirty bills to provide general
Federal aid to the schools were futilely introduced in six
sessions of three Congressses. Committees of both Houses held
five separate hearings, at which an estimated 400 witnesses
testified, over periods totaling at least two solid months, their
testimony running to something like 4,000 printed pages. Two
of those bills were overwhelmingly passed by the U.S. Senate.
Yet at no time did the House Committee in charge of such
measures see fit to allow the House of Representatives itself
to vote on a single one of them.

The probability is strong that if it had done so, the hard-
pressed elementary and secondary public schools of the country would long since have had some form of Federal assistance,
and Congress would by now have had ample opportunity to
perfect the program and eliminate whatever weaknesses
emerged. But whether or not a bill would have passed, and
whether or not that would have been desirable, the significant
fact is that a single small group of sometimes squabbling,
sometimes wholly dominated, men were able to deny, without
challenge, the right of decision to more than 400 of their
colleagues.

If all such measures were buried in committee from 1945
through 1950, they were not even allowed a stillbirth in the
four years that followed. Assuming the chairmanship of the
full committee in 1951, on Lesinski's death, Barden simply
would not allow the subject to be discussed. He decided when
the Committee would meet, and there were sometimes gaps
of two months between sessions. If there was a possibility that
he might be embarrassed by a shrewd maneuver, he would
go fishing for days, and no one dared take the chair in his
absence. In the single Congress that the Republicans controlled, 1953–1954, the chairmanship fell to Representative
McConnell, a far milder operator. But the effect was the same.
Federal aid to the schools was a painful and divisive issue,

and both McConnell and the newly installed Eisenhower Administration were for letting all such issues lie. For those of a let-well-enough-alone approach to political life, few institutions in the world can be as soothing as a Congressional committee.

5

Fabian Arts of the Floor

With all the busts of the great that adorn the Capitol's Statuary Hall, room might logically have been found for the Roman General called Fabius Cunctator, or Fabius the Delayer, for his talent in harrying an adversary to death without actually joining battle. The exception of his foreign presence in this all-American company might be allowed, since his spirit of delay-and-conquer already pervades Capitol Hill, even as it pervaded, in his time, the Punic battlefields. And nowhere more so than in the two legislative chambers themselves, though it is only fair to observe that in the House that spirit is more excessive in appearance than in reality.

Occasionally a visitor to the Capitol arrives in the gallery at a moment of high drama and achievement, but the odds are against it. It is vastly more probable that, in the House of

Representatives, he will look down on a disjointed scene, chaotic without being exciting, which he will scarcely be able to follow and which will not inspire him to make the effort. Of the 435 members, perhaps not more than 50 or 60 will be in their seats, some reading newspapers, others buzzing conversationally; few, if any, giving an ear to their colleague, who from the well of the sloping chamber has just interrupted his remarks to ask the Speaker for order. From his lofty, high-backed chair at the pinnacle of a triple dais, the Speaker mechanically raps his gavel and announces, "The House will be in order." But the change he produces is not perceptible. Members continue to drift in and out of the doors between the cloak rooms and the huge and handsome walnut-paneled chamber. One stops to greet a friend en route, another drops into a seat beside a colleague for a brief exchange of business or personal chitchat.

The chances are the members miss little by not listening to what has been emanating from the well. On a typical day, following the Chaplain's prayer and the reading of the previous day's *Journal*, a session—I have a real one in mind—starts off like this: A member from Texas, the Honorable John Dowdy, rises, requesting permission to revise and extend his remarks in the *Congressional Record*, which means permission to insert a speech he has not made and will not ever make, along with the full text of an editorial from the Lufkin (Texas) *News*. No objection is heard because no one could care less and because no member would dream of endangering this common privilege. He is followed by Representative Tom Murray of Tennessee, seeking unanimous consent to have a bill fixing the words to be used on stamps in the Canal Zone re-referred from the Committee on Post Office and Civil Service to the Committee on Merchant Marine and Fisheries. Having obtained this boon, the gentleman from Tennessee is in turn succeeded by Barratt O'Hara, the gentleman from Illinois. He, too, seeks permission to extend his remarks in the *Record* in order to carry on a controversy with the Honorable Joe D. Waggonner, Jr., of Louisiana on the question of whether or not the Roman Emperor Lucius Septimius Severus had Negro blood. For several days he has been trying by trumpeting the case of Severus to refute the highly publicized remark of a world-traveling Senator that Negroes have shown no ability to govern themselves. Triumphantly he now cites as his authority none other than John Gunther, hoping thereby to silence his opponent's contention that if the story was true, it would have been mentioned by Gibbon, whose silence on the point would be like "a modern historian failing to note that . . . Fidel Castro was, in reality, Carmen Miranda with a beard." So it goes.

Perhaps the easiest thing in the world is to pick up a copy of the *Congressional Record,* any issue, and locate a ream or two of such foolishness. But it is a cheap accomplishment if it is used to evaluate the quality of Congress. For a good part, or a bad part, of what goes into the *Record* is not spoken on the floor at all and is strictly intended for home consumption. In itself this is not altogether admirable, at $86 of taxpayers' money per printed page; in a sense it is even a deception of the folks back home. They may have a hunch that their Congressman did not write the speech attributed to him in the reprint from the *Record,* which they have received, postage-free, in their mail; but they do think he has at least delivered it, perhaps to a rapt chamber and a breathless gallery. Nevertheless, the argument can, and is, made that permission to "revise and extend" does save time on the floor of Congress.[1]

There is much room to doubt, however, whether, in this

---

[1] Often the practice is carried to an absurd length by allowing members five days after a major bill has been passed to "revise and extend" remarks about it which they never made, and which might well have been refuted if they had. Unlike most of us, Congressmen can be scintillating long after the argument is over and still get credit for it.

superficial way, Congress really wants to save time. For behind
the façade of floor proceedings tactics are worked out, for or
against legislation, and often enough the official consumption
of time is, for one side or the other, just what is wanted. It
allows for maneuvering. If this were not so, it is hard to believe that Congress, especially the House, would not long ago
have introduced electric voting machinery, which has proved
its practical worth in close to half the state legislatures. Instead, repeated quorum calls and roll calls, endlessly droned
out by the clerk, are allowed to take a staggering amount of
Congressional time. In the second session of the 87th Congress,
for example, the House sat for close to 657 hours, of which
something like 163 hours, or very close to 25 percent, were
given to finding out whether a quorum was present or to voting
by roll call. Electricity would have done the job in something
like forty-one hours, allowing fifteen minutes warning time for
each roll call and two minutes for the operation itself, and
releasing one hundred twenty-two hours, or something like
twenty-four additional legislative days, for other business. But
the late Speaker Rayburn, like most House officials before
him, brushed aside the proposal for "instant voting," deeming
"the old way of calling the roll . . . quite a lot better." For
members who could see themselves at some time or another
relying on delay in the course of a floor fight, the Speaker's
preference was understandable, and since almost everyone
was of this company, the proposal's defense has been left to a
few congenital reformers.

When the House at last gets down to debating a bill, however, it should be said that the argument is limited in time,
kept pretty well to the point, and often highly informed. As
a rule the chief debate is conducted with the House sitting
as the Committee of the Whole, a convenient fiction that allows
the body to function with 100 members present rather than the
technical majority of 219. Under its special rules, moreover,

time-consuming roll calls are dispensed with, all votes being taken by voice, by standing count (division), or by tellers who check off the members as they file through the well, first those in favor, then those against.

The usual course is for the bill's sponsor, once it has emerged from committee, obtained a rule from the Rules Committee, and been reached on the calendar, to rise and say, "Mr. Speaker, I move that the House resolve itself into the Committee of the Whole House for the State of the Union to consider H. R. 102." The Speaker then steps down from the dais, first designating any Representative he chooses to serve as chairman, and a timekeeper prepares to limit speakers in accordance with the rules agreed upon for debating this particular bill.[2]

The bill's floor manager, usually the chairman of the parent committee, and the floor manager for the opposition between them parcel out the agreed time among their followers until the fixed limit for the general debate has been reached. After that anyone may speak five minutes on an amendment, but just to keep things from getting too efficient, a member who does not have a real amendment in mind but nevertheless wants to talk may offer a *pro forma* amendment. This consists in moving to "strike out the last word," or the last two words, or as many words as he likes, a meaningless proposal, after which he may proceed to discuss any phase of the bill he chooses for the allotted five minutes.

Once the hierarchy of the House is committed to a bill—

[2] These ground rules have been worked out by the Rules Committee and passed by the House just prior to the debate. The House may reject them, of course, but it rarely does, even when it is asked to swallow a "gag rule," which provides for a straight yes-or-no decision, with no amendments allowed. If a majority does vote against the proposed rule, the bill has to go back to Rules, which means that it is probably dead for the session, making one more way in which a measure can be fatally sidetracked without a vote on its substance.

that is, the chairman of the parent committee, the chairman of Rules, the Majority Leader, and, above all, the Speaker— the measure is likely to go flying through the House itself with dazzling speed, especially if it is a creature of the powerful Appropriations Committee. Bills from that source are privileged. They are not subject to amendment, and the average Congressman does not even pretend to pass judgment on them. In the closing days of the first session of the Eighty-seventh Congress, five such bills, totaling close to *sixteen billion dollars* in appropriations, whirled through the floor processes of the House in four days. It should be remembered, of course, that by the time the full chamber gets bills of this sort, much of the controversy has been squeezed out of them by time and compromise, and by now passage has become an urgent matter of sustaining the very flow of government.

The controls that *can* force speed in the House—a powerful top echelon and self-imposed curbs on debate—are notably absent in the Senate. That body invests in each of its hundred members an astonishing degree of power to block action and operates to an even more astonishing degree on the hope of unanimity. A single member could, if he wished, paralyze the Senate by regularly objecting to the many moves that require unanimous consent: allowing a committee to meet while the Senate is in session, agreeing to limit debate, and permitting immediate passage of personal and noncontroversial bills.[3] All that can keep him from acting the complete nuisance in this

[3] What seems like a noncontroversial bill to 99 Senators often seems extremely controversial to the hundredth. Senator Taft once refused unanimous consent to a bill for exterminating Washington's starlings on the ground that the birds killed Japanese beetles and the bill proposed no alternative method for keeping the beetle population in hand. The Committee on the District of Columbia was forced to put in long hours discussing the question, but the starlings are still around.

fashion, if he is so inclined, is the fear of retaliation and the likelihood of a quarantine imposed by his peers. Cut off from all those favors that a member needs in order to serve his constituents, he would quickly understand that unless he changed his tack, his usefulness in the Senate would be limited and his days accordingly numbered.

It is only this informal give-and-take, this general willingness to yield when little or nothing is lost by graciousness, this constant exchange of favors, that allows the Senate to operate at all. On its highest level this very personal system presents a model of forebearance and gracious flexibility; on a middle level, a formal "courtesy" so stylized as to suggest the stately courting ritual of flamingoes; and on its lowest level a subjection to minority, or even individual, whim that approaches self-paralysis.

Looking down from the Senate gallery, as we did from the House, we get a markedly different impression. The chamber is even visually quieter in tone, with a hundred desks, in the style of 1819, in place of the crowded seats required to accommodate the 435 Representatives. The Vice President's desk on the rostrum is at a much lower elevation than the Speaker's in the House, subtly indicating perhaps the difference between the relationship of Senators to their nominal presiding officer and Representatives to their very real one. The wall panels of cream marble, flanked by columns of red Levanto marble, seem elegantly appropriate to what has long been regarded as the world's most exclusive club.

At a given moment one may find even fewer members on duty in the chamber than was the case on the other side of the Capitol. On the day Senator Clark held forth on the need for Congressional reform, a distasteful subject to many, he could not help remarking on the sparseness of his audience:

> If one looks around the Chamber of the Senate now, he will see what might be called normal Senate attendance. The very

able junior Senator from Ohio [Sen. YOUNG] is waiting for
an opportunity to make his speech. In the chair at present is
a very able freshman Senator [Sen. McINTYRE].[4] In addition, I am present, and there is also present the new Senator
from New Mexico [Sen. MEACHEM], who is holding down,
with great ability and some persistence, the seat of the minority leader, who, I presume, is off on other business which he
considers more important than listening again to the senior
Senator from Pennsylvania on a subject with respect to which
the distinguished minority leader does not find himself in
agreement with the views of the senior Senator from Pennsylvania.

If the attendance was normal, Clark's style was even more
so. Although engaged in an unorthodox assault on "The Establishment," the senior Senator from Pennsylvania, as he tradi-
tionally referred to himself, was observing the customary
manners. Other Senators were not only given their formal
designations, even in the most passing reference, but these
were generally prefaced by one or another of the stock adjec-
tives of compliment that have become so threadbare in the
Senate that they have meaning only when they are omitted.
Mr. Young was "the very able junior Senator from Ohio" (he
was seventy-three at the time but junior to his colleague from
Ohio in point of service in the Senate, the only criterion in
Congress). The absent Senator Dirksen was "the distinguished
minority leader," whom Clark was sarcastically taking to task.
Senator Barkley, who always had a genial tongue in his cheek,
once laid down the rule for the benefit of new members that

---

[4] In the absence from the chamber of both the Vice President
and the President pro tempore, the chair is often assigned to a
freshman Senator. The theory is that for long stretches the chairmanship is a chore, rightly to be performed by new members.
There is little risk of his making mistakes, since in all rulings he
is guided by the parliamentarian, who sits just below him. He
has no qualms about taking the parliamentarian's directives, because the Vice President and President pro tempore do exactly the
same thing.

a Senator who is thought to be stupid should always be referred to as "the able, learned and distinguished Senator"; one who is *known* to be stupid, as "the *very* able, learned and distinguished Senator."

At the bottom of this elaborate feeling for Senatorial sensibilities is in part a real concern against allowing what Senator Morse once described as that "nasty debate that one can hear in many parliamentary bodies around the world," and that in his judgment destroys their effectiveness. Probably more basic is the simple fact that an offended Senator may some day use his one-man leverage on the Senate machinery to make grave trouble for a personal bill or local project that is vitally necessary to his offender.

Fortifying this natural concern is the rule of both Houses forbidding language that imputes unworthy motives to a colleague, even of the other House, or is otherwise insulting. A violator of the rule who does not quickly withdraw the offending remarks can be forced to take his seat and have his comments expunged from the record. But as may readily be imagined, where there's a will to insult, there's a way. The amusing case cited by Bertram M. Gross in his book, *The Legislative Struggle,* was at least a short cut. "I wish to know if there is any way under the parliamentary rules of the Senate," came an inquiry from the floor, "whereby one member may refer to another as a wilful, malicious liar?" Under threat of having to take his seat, the speaker quickly reverted to propriety: "The charges made by the Senator from Michigan, I will say, in parliamentary language, are as much without foundation as it is possible for any charges to be." Much more elaborate was the technique employed by Senator Williams of Delaware when taken to task for an extreme denunciation of Representative Adam Clayton Powell. Denying Senator Morse's charge that he had violated the rule, Williams pleaded:

I did not discuss this person's conduct in the House of Representatives. I never said one word yesterday, nor will I today, about this person having relatives on the public payroll who are not working. I am not calling attention to it today.

I will not mention the fact that his wife is on his payroll, nor will I raise any question as to whether she does any work. Neither will I say that he is not fulfilling his duties and is guilty of a great deal of absenteeism. . . .

The chief point of difference between the two Houses of Congress is the Senate's low tolerance of controls. While the House is often at the mercy of its autonomous committee barons, the course of action, once a bill reaches the floor, is pretty rigidly fixed, as we have seen. But in the Senate the opposite is true. Its Rules Committee is one of its least influential groups and even the chairmen of its standing committees, powerful as they are, can be overcome by determined action. But on the floor, the Senate as an institution subjects itself to the whim of 100 all-powerful individuals, any one of whom may obtrude on a debate, no matter how important it is, to discuss some totally irrelevant subject. Once he takes the floor, a wistful majority leader once observed, "nobody but Almighty God can interrupt him—and the Lord never seems to take any notice."

In general parliamentary practice the rule is that all discussion shall be germane, that it must with reasonable directness be addressed to the pending subject. Since an unfortunate ruling of the Chair in 1872, to the effect that failure to speak to the point is not out of order, no such relevancy was required in the United States Senate for ninety years—until a modified brake was applied in January, 1964. The result is that debate in that chamber, eloquent and highly informed as it is in its best moments, is often marred by rambling interruptions and endless delay—one reason, by the way, that televising its proceedings has not been found practical.

Testifying before a Senate committee considering the defects of Congress, in 1951, Senator Hendrickson of New Jersey put the problem with some originality: "Consider for a moment that epitome of American efficiency, the automobile assembly line," he said. "Can we conceive of the engineers, right at the point where the chassis are attached to the frames, all of a sudden starting to assemble refrigerators and leaving the half-assembled cars to wait?" Not at all, but in the midst of a Senate debate on an appropriation bill, "someone will start producing refrigerators—in the form of a digression on grain to India, the Missouri River, the MacArthur affair, or a tribute to National Song and Dance Week."

Twelve years after Hendrickson's apt metaphor a randomly selected issue of the *Congressional Record* (July 18, 1963) shows no improvement of the Senate assembly line. "Mr. President," asks the Majority Whip, "may the Senate now proceed with the unfinished business?" which happens to be a bill to amend the Tariff Act. "Without objection, it is so ordered," replies the Vice President, according to ritual. Whereupon the Republican Senator from Delaware rises, a bit playfully, to let his colleagues know first that the Department of Health, Education, and Welfare is throwing away taxpayers' money on research grants for studies of such matters as "physiological adaptation in the Mexican free-tailed bat." Next Senator Metcalf of Montana gives a conservation speech on the effect that poorly planned highway construction can have on streams, fish, and wildlife. He is followed by a short interpolation from Senator Bartlett of Alaska, who wants his colleagues to know that the approaching eclipse of the sun will be total for a longer period at Talkeetna, Alaska, than anywhere else on the continent, that "it is not yet too late to secure an airplane ticket to Anchorage, Alaska, and to drive out to this charming and small community of Talkeetna, not far distant."

All this time Senator Humphrey, the Majority Whip, has been waiting patiently to move ahead with the amendment to the Tariff Act. But before the chamber gets around to this pending business, he has still to hear Senator Robertson of Virginia on compulsory arbitration, civil rights, and balance of payments; Senator Keating of New York on Jewish military personnel with the American forces in Saudi Arabia and the observance of Captive Nations Week in Rochester; Senator Javits of New York on the Jubilee Celebration of the Rockefeller Foundation and the Securities and Exchange Commission's study of the stock market; Senator Dominick of Colorado and several others on the Cuban Menace Today; and Senator Hayden of Arizona presenting a conference report on an appropriations bill. Nobody is in the least bothered by the fact that none of this has the slightest connection with the business officially before the Senate at the moment. Indeed, somewhere along the line the Whip himself has managed to squeeze in the introduction of a couple of visiting Brazilian congressmen, with appropriate remarks of welcome.

At long last the Senator from Virginia rises to discuss the "pending bill." The Senate sticks to it for all of twenty minutes before Senator Morse of Oregon breaks in to conduct with Senator Miller of Iowa a brief exchange on foreign aid and to introduce an important amendment to existing law on that subject. Ambling along, constantly diverted like a ten-year-old on his way to school, the chamber finally returns to the business in hand, and some time in the course of the afternoon's meandering the amendment is passed. Had it been a highly controversial bill the game might well have gone on for days, at a cost estimated by Senator Humphrey some years ago, of around $33,000 a day. At one point during the debate on the Fair Labor Standards bill, the Senate was in session for nine continuous hours without giving more than an hour and a quarter to that hotly contested, intermittently argued, measure.

In the summer of 1963, historians may note, Senators took formal notice that their debate included what one of them described as "a lot of guff." A recommendation was thereupon made to the Rules Committee that such guff be confined to the "morning hour," usually from twelve to two. Nothing was expected to come of this daring plan for relevancy in the afternoon. On the contrary, when it reached the ear of Senator Everett Dirksen of Illinois, that powerful Minority Leader made the admittedly germane comment: "Ha, ha, ha! And I might add, ho, ho, ho!" For those who might think this a bit cryptic, he went on to explain that in the Senate "the only weapon which the minority has to protect itself" is the utterly unrestrained right of a member to talk when and as he is moved by duty, spirit, or whim.

Nevertheless, on January 23 under the pressure of mounting public criticism, the Senate voted 57 to 25 to be relevant for three hours a day—unless a member specifically obtained permission to wander. Senator Dirksen sadly noted this step "down the road to tyranny," but Senator Russell, who likewise fought the change, was less exercised. The resolution which had been brought in by Senator Pastore of Rhode Island could easily be circumvented. An amendment to any bill under discussion, he pointed out, can be as nongermane as a Senator pleases, and under its cover, he may oratorically wander as far afield as ever.

It is not always easy to say where the loquacity of Senators ceases to be merely dilatory and becomes a full-blown filibuster. By and large, the difference between "extended debate" and filibustering lies in the degree of hope that may be entertained by the practitioners. If a few more votes are needed to win and there is some chance of getting them—by persuasion, pressure from an aroused public, or negotiation—

then clearly delay by extended debate is a sound and proper strategy. In the case of a genuine filibuster the impossibility of winning by vote is clear from the start; the intention is simply to talk, without let or hindrance, for weeks if necessary, until the proponents of the hated measure, in the majority though they are, give up in order to get on with the business of the Senate.

Where the aim is truly to win doubters to the cause, the speakers are naturally likely to concentrate on the matter in hand, however prolonged their talk. The filibusterer, on the other hand, need not be finicky. He must go on long after he and his allies have exhausted the subject, and in any case he does not feel bound to keep to the point since he is not out to convince but to obstruct. Thus Senator Holt of West Virginia thought nothing of reading *Aesop's Fables* to a chamber bent on passing a coal conservation bill. Another Senator held forth on the life cycle of the butterfly when control of public utilities was before the house. Others have passed the hours reading baseball scores and analyzing the Constitution, article by article, and "Pitchfork Ben" Tillman one of the Senate's great demagogues, threatened to treat his fellows to a reading of Byron's *Childe Harold*. The feats of the dubiously great Huey Long in this type of endeavor are too well known to bear repeating, and in any case his best performance has since been surpassed several times, in tenacity if not in color. A fellow-Southerner, Strom Thurmond of South Carolina, conducted a one-man "educational debate," as he called it, on the 1957 Civil Rights Act which ran nearly nine hours longer than Long's record of 15 hours, 30 minutes.

With politicians more conscious of their "public images" than they once were, filibusterers now tend to stray less exotically from the business at hand than they used to, but at best their act is not inspiring. Describing a one-man filibuster, the least harmful of the species because the soonest over, Donald R. Matthews in his "U.S. Senators and Their World" catches the quality of the thing:

> It is near the close of a long, hot session. The solons have long since decided to adjourn and go home. Then one of them begins to talk. As night approaches, his voice becomes an inaudible croak. He begins to totter for he is not permitted to sit down or lean upon his desk and he is not young. If too many of the other men leave the room, the speaker demands a quorum. Bells ring throughout the Capitol and the absent members slowly return to the chamber. The call permits him to rest his rasping voice for half an hour. So some members remain in the chamber while others stretch out on the couches in the cloak rooms or sleep on folding cots set up nearby. And the man keeps on talking. Finally, after interminable hours of mumbled words, the one-man talkathon ends. Is this the most powerful democratic legislature in the world?

It is wrong to think of the filibuster as a peculiarly Southern contribution to the folkways of the Senate. Such gods of the Northern liberal pantheon as George Norris and the elder La Follette used it freely, if not happily, notably to thwart President Wilson's proposal to arm American merchant ships in 1917. In the same proud category, Senator Morse of Oregon gave what seems to have been the most rugged solo performance in the history of the Senate. Filibustering against an off-shore oil bill in 1954, Morse actually held the floor two hours less than Thurmond was to do a few years later, but while Thurmond would enjoy the interruption of a number of quorum calls, during which he could retire to the rest room, Morse was on his feet the entire twenty-two hours.[5]

All the same, association of the filibuster with the Senators

---

[5] For those who appreciate such data, Thurmond consumed three glasses of milk and a pitcher of orange juice in the course of his ordeal; Morse had occasional servings of bouillon, coffee, and tea, munched candy and crackers from time to time, and sucked ice.

of the South is natural, since they have made the most consistent use of it in the course of a century-long rear-guard
action to reverse the decision of the Civil War. To this very
writing they have also been the most successful, using the
device not only to ward off laws that would alter the status
of the Negro in the South, but to prevent, year after year,
any change in the Senate rules themselves that would make
it easier to shut off such debate. In the Eighty-eighth Congress
alone, the Senate wasted its first twenty legislative days in a
fruitless attempt to overcome the Southerners' filibuster of a
proposal to limit filibusters.

To be sure, it has been possible, since 1917, to invoke
cloture, that is, finally to force an end to debate. But the
machinery provided for the purpose is clumsy, and resistance
is great. Of the twenty-seven attempts that have been made
since the rule was adopted in 1917, only five were successful.
Of the twenty-two failures, nine were in connection with civil
rights legislation, which has yet to be benefited by the cloture
rule.

If it seems hard to believe that the Senate cannot be brought
to vote for eliminating so palpably unfair a device as the
filibuster, it need only be borne in mind that in the back of
every Senator's head is the thought that some day, driven
into a corner, he may be deeply grateful for this last weapon
of a minority. On this basis it has been defended by such
stalwart liberals as Norris, who called it "one of the greatest
weapons against wrong and oppression the members of this
body possess."

Yet the fact remains that even if the cloture rule were
strengthened to allow a simple majority of the membership
to end debate, the right of the minority to state its case would
not be curtailed. In any change of the rule, guarantees would
certainly be retained to forbid the invoking of the rule until
a fixed and ample period of debate had already run and to

allow a fixed additional time for final arguments. If the minority wants *more* than this opportunity, if it seeks simply and finally to prevail over the majority, then it carries close to absurdity the philosophical case for a legislative minority's rights. In the specific case of legislation for racial equality, involving the most fundamental rights of a large minority of the nation's citizens, a plea for filibustering in the name of minority rights tumbles into absurdity altogether and need not be dignified by philosophic argument. At best it might be said that if any senator or bloc of senators is to be invested with such power, it would be better to give them the veto at once; that would at least save time and spare their colleagues the pain of enduring wave after wave of verbiage offered for no more reason than to induce them at last to cry "Hold, enough!" Senator Henry Cabot Lodge, the Elder, summed it up some seventy years ago: "To vote without debating is perilous, but to debate and never vote is imbecile."

Should a bill survive all the delaying tactics open to its opponents, it is then free to struggle against amendment on the floor, which is sometimes proper and helpful, sometimes harmful to a serious degree, and often enough fatal. The British House of Commons is stricter about accepting amendments from the floor than the American Congress, and most Representatives and Senators freely concede that the place to write a bill is in the committee. But if one's own bill has been treated roughly in that inner council, or if one has vainly tried, as leader of the minority in the committee, to hamstring a bill before it is reported, amendment on the floor may represent the last chance to prevail.

In view of the overriding ways of some Congressional committee chairmen, discussed in an earlier chapter, this spirit might be wholly commendable but for the extremes to which the amending process itself is sometimes carried, especially in the Senate. With the same antipathy to germaneness that they show in debate, Senators think nothing of adding totally irrelevant sections to a measure, often more far-reaching than the bill itself. Sometimes bills are loaded in this way deliberately in order to kill them, sometimes to sweeten them for members who might otherwise vote against them, and sometimes simply to give the so-called amendment a free ride on the back of legislation already guaranteed strong support.

To a layman it may seem incredible that practically unopposed bills to put up new American embassies in several countries were twice defeated for reasons having nothing whatever to do with the subject. On the first occasion the Senate attached a rider calling for equal rights for women. The second time around, it tacked on a rider concerning the collection of fees by agents in war-damage claims. Neither "amendment" had a blessed thing to do with embassy buildings, but they caused both bills to be beaten. Similarly, Senator Langer of North Dakota once tried, unsuccessfully, to kill a bill repealing the tax on oleomargarine by loading it with an antilynching amendment.

In his days as Majority Leader, Lyndon Johnson once infuriated the Southern contingent by obtaining unanimous consent to take up a wholly noncontroversial bill dealing with funds for a military base, then announcing that it was subject to amendment, and proceeding to tack on to it what amounted to a substantial civil rights bill. In this way the hostile Judiciary Committee, which would have buried the amendment had it come to it as a separate bill, was circumvented and a modest civil rights measure was passed. Here the civil libertarian might have felt that the institution of the rider paid off, but to anyone concerned with more than the tactics of the moment it was a freakish way to legislate, and the Southerners were justified in crying foul.

As a rule the results of this misuse of the amending process are more negative—and are intended to be so. Western Senators once used riders calling for the remonetization of silver to defeat bills on other subjects, hoping eventually in this way to get what they wanted. In the same way Congressmen of the past decade have tied civil rights riders to legislation ranging from Federal aid to the schools, as we shall see, to a bill dealing with boiled peanuts. The results have been almost always to kill the bill rather than to pass the rider.

Carrying the procedure a step farther, Representative Hosmer of California tauntingly inserted in the *Congressional Record* (as an "extension of remarks") a brief discussion of how members may "make good" on campaign pledges they regret having made: by all means introduce the bills you have promised, but then load them down with enough millstones to sink a barge.

> The specific technique is to put a promise in bill form, making sure the bill also is loaded up with lots more items so unpalatable to large numbers of legislators they must vote against it. The skilled political gamesman can achieve an additional unpopularity bonus for the bill by leaving out numerous other items, the omission of which is wholly unpalatable to another bloc of legislators. Almost surely the bill will be defeated and the haunt exorcised. In the process the political gamesman has appeared to work with selfless devotion to produce on his promise. He remains glorious in defeat. . . .

The possibilities for killing a bill on the floor, short of defeating it forthrightly by vote, are not at all exhausted by dilatory maneuvers that may worry it to death, by filibusters, and by hedging it with such patently antagonizing riders that it is doomed before it starts. Of the few other methods that have been provided, the gentlest, as suggested in Chapter I, is a motion to recommit. Often this move to return a bill to committee is accompanied by instructions to make certain changes in it, too complicated, presumably, to be made on the floor. The maneuver is particularly appealing in connection with a bill which a majority of members, perhaps for perfectly sound reasons, do not want, but which has enough appeal among the voters back home to make outright opposition a little risky. No harm whatever is done by bucking such a bill back to a standing committee on the pretext of wanting to see it strengthened or clarified. Where amendment is not the real aim and an adverse vote is dangerous, recommittal is a perfect out. No one is under the illusion that the committee, unless a time limit is fixed in the instructions, will embarrass anyone by returning a bill to the calendar in the same session.

A comparison between the difficulty of shutting off a filibuster in the Senate and the ease with which any matter may be tabled illustrates nicely the Congressional emphasis on the negative. The filibuster itself, making action impossible, is of course the ultimate in negation, and under the present rules nothing much can be done about it. But when a move is made to table an amendment, or a bill for that matter, debate is instantly cut off and a vote taken on the motion. If it carries, the matter is dead right then and there, showing again how much easier it is to give a bill the *coup de grace* than to help it on its way.

One of the most brutal, as well as curious, ways of doing a measure to death on the floor is the device of moving to strike out the enacting clause. This motion, which must be brought to a vote after extremely limited debate, simply beheads a measure, as explained in the first chapter, by dropping the very words that would make it a law. It is not resorted to often, and only when the House is sitting as a Committee of the Whole. That means that it must be voted on again by the House itself, but it does serve to force the issue and, again, in a wholly negative way. If the motion is passed by the full House, the bill is dead; if the motion is lost, the bill is by no means passed but merely continues to go its hazardous way through the mine field.

Even after a bill *is* passed—and this is unique in legislative practice—a motion is in order to reconsider the vote just taken. In theory only a supporter of the bill can make such a motion, the idea being that he and others like him may suddenly have seen the light or otherwise discovered reasons to switch and should be given the chance. In practice, however, it is a simple matter, unless the voting is likely to be extremely close, for an opponent formally to vote *for* the bill, or a supporter to vote against it, just so that he will be free to move reconsideration. There is a time limit for reconsideration—one day in the House, two in the Senate—but that is long enough for great pressures to be brought to bear on those who are not firmly committed. To forestall this danger a bill's managers usually see to it that one of their own followers makes a *pro forma* motion to reconsider immediately after the original vote, while their majority is still on the floor to beat it down. But once in a while, after a close decision, a few hitherto absent members of the opposition are rushed in, and defeat once more is snatched from the jaws of victory.

6

School Bills on the Floor

Between disaster in the Eighty-first Congress and emergency efforts in the Eighty-fourth, the issue of Federal aid to the schools seems to have been regarded in the House Committee on Education and Labor as a subject in doubtful taste. In particular, all mention of parochial schools, so explosive in 1949 and 1950, was taboo. Two observers report the comment of a Republican member who broke the rule:

> I made a speech on the floor about it. When I came back, Sam McConnell said to me, "That's one thing I wouldn't have said if I were you." I said, "Well, I believe it." And he said, "I know, but that's one subject we shy away from." [1]

It was not that the need for new school facilities had appreciably shrunk or that public interest in Federal aid had

[1] Frank J. Munger and Richard F. Fenno, Jr. in *National Politics and Federal Aid to Education*, p. 154.

faded. On the contrary, between 1948 and 1955 public-opinion polls showed a steady increase of those favoring some sort of Federal help, roughly from 61 percent to 68 percent. Testing for confirmation, Rep. Frelinghuysen, a Committee member, sent a questionnaire to his own strongly Republican district in New Jersey. Although that wealthy state stood to contribute more to a Federal-aid program than it would get back, approval ran as high as 70 percent. Both party platforms in the campaign of 1952 had paid formal tribute to Federal-aid legislation, and both nominees for the Presidency had pledged themselves to seek it. And by way of response on Capitol Hill no fewer than fifty-three bills and resolutions to this end, many of them duplicating each other, were introduced in the Eighty-third Congress.

But Congressional promoters of an aid program knew the nature of their machine and once more sought a way out by indirection. Not a single one of these half a hundred measures found its way to the floor of either House. Instead, just as the Congress of Jackson's day hoped to help the schools by dispersing the Treasury's surplus from the sale of Western lands, some in the Congresses of the early 1950s hoped to use Federal income from offshore oil lands. To several bills calling for the national acquisition of these rich tidelands, amendments were added providing that the expected revenues were to be turned into grants-in-aid for education. One such oil-for-education rider actually got through the Senate, but the House, with its much stricter rules of relevance, challenged its germaneness and got it eliminated in a conference committee of the two chambers. The Federal government got its revenues but the oil lit no lamps of knowledge.

The result was that, when the Eighty-fourth Congress convened in January of 1955, the need was as great as ever; indirect methods had failed, and the situation was almost where it had been ten years earlier. "Almost," because one aspect of the problem had changed. Eight months earlier the Supreme Court had handed down its historic decision barring racial segregation in the public schools. As far as the legislative prospects for Federal aid to education were concerned, it was unhappily to be a change for the worse. A determined minority would now fight off all Federal aid for fear it would be used to force a quick showdown on the Court's decision; there would be no grants, it feared, without compliance. And for a determined minority the machinery of Congress is made to order.

Amended to Death—1956

In a special message to Congress early in February, President Eisenhower led off the campaign by urging a school-aid program of stunningly modest proportions. Calling for loans by way of Federal purchase of school bonds and limited grants for the neediest districts only, the proposal, which was attributed to Oveta Culp Hobby, Secretary of Health, Welfare, and Education, was described by Senator Kerr of Oklahoma as "conceived by investment bankers and dedicated to the money lenders." More diplomatically, the NEA's President Carr paid tribute to Mr. Eisenhower for treating the schools as "part of the state of the Union" before going on to note that "while we admired and applauded the viewpoint and policy that the President had put into his message, we just could not honestly face the Congress of the United States and say that the specific legislation could do the job or would even, with some exceptions, be a useful piece of legislation."

At the time President Eisenhower's proposal was made, more than twenty other school bills had already been dropped in the hopper of the month-old Congress. Picked out of all of these by the House Committee on Education and Labor for serious attention was H. R. 7535, introduced by Representative Augustine Kelley, a Democrat from Pennsylvania. Stronger than the Administration proposal, the Kelley bill was nevertheless a limited measure of an emergency character. The appropriation requested was modest; the grants, which were to be matched by the states, were to be limited to four years; and the funds could be used for construction only. It was to achieve the historic distinction of actually emerging from committee—*but* too late in the session for any action on the floor.

What held up the Kelley bill was the adroit and elaborate foot-dragging of Chairman Graham Barden, who had always favored school-aid legislation, but not much. Barden insisted on having the full Committee take over the hearings, and the deep-furrowed ground was ploughed again—at excruciating length. Refusing to fix regular meeting days or to put any time limit on the questioning of the fifty-two witnesses, the chairman managed to stretch the ceremony out over a period of twelve weeks. Meanwhile, nerves grew taut and passions rose. At the end of May some fifteen insurgents on the Committee staged a revolt against their chairman's dilatory tactics. "I spent five months here last year on a bill that we suddenly threw out the window," protested Roy Wier, a Minnesota Democrat and leader of the group. "And if we are not going to pass out a school bill, let's get on to the wage-hour bill." But Barden still made the rules, and he was easily a match for the rebels.

It was eight weeks later that a vote was taken, and not before tempers had flared explosively. At one point Representative Powell tried to attach an antisegregation amendment whereby no funds could go to districts that refused to build racially integrated schools. According to Representative Bailey, a West Virginia Democrat and a leading advocate of Federal aid, the amendment would without question kill the bill, and he challenged the genuineness of Powell's interest. In the exchange the gentlemen from New York charged the gentleman from West Virginia with "a lie," and the gentleman from West

Virginia countered with a right to the jaw of the gentleman from New York. As usual, of course, the amenities were restored with a handshake and an extra larding of Congressional compliment. But the amendment was voted down, 17 to 10. Whereupon Powell served notice that he would try again when and if the bill got to the floor. He was undisturbed by the fact that some of those on the Committee who voted with him for the amendment were strongly against the bill itself and were pretty clearly hoping to make use of him.

With the House all set to adjourn on Tuesday, August 2, the Kelley bill was reported out on Thursday, July 28. Since it had not the ghost of a chance to be called up for debate, the historic nature of the occasion was diluted. However, since this was just the end of a session, not of a Congress, the bill was still alive when the House convened again the following January. In the inevitable maneuvering and delay it did not reach the floor until June 28, exactly eleven months from the time, not when it had been introduced, but when it had been reported out by the Committee. For five of these months, to be sure, Congress was not in session; the remaining six went into efforts by the bill's supporters to line up votes against the Powell Amendment and to get the bill through the roadblock of the Rules Committee, whose chairman, as we shall see, had little fondness for such measures. All the same, this was to be the first time in the twentieth century that the House of Representatives would actually debate the question of general aid to the schools. The Senate, which had debated it often and favorably in the past, now stood aside, unwilling to engage in a bruising and fruitless fight over segregation unless the bill should at last get through the other chamber.

The religious issue, which had proved so damaging six years before, had been neatly bypassed. The bill was for construction only, and no one had yet suggested that Federal funds should be spent to build parochial school buildings. Augustine

Kelley, its sponsor, was himself a devout Catholic. And John McCormack, then Democratic majority leader, took occasion to praise the "unselfish, statesmanlike attitude" of the champions of private and parochial schools for having "refrained from any action that might impede passage of this bill even though it will bring no direct benefit to their schools."

All in all, prospects seemed fair during the six hours of general debate that had been agreed upon for the bill. Democrats and Republicans alike were giving it good support. Opposition was heard only from Southern Democrats, fearful of a new weapon for the integrationists, and those extreme anti-Eisenhower conservatives on the Republican side of the aisle who habitually damned Federal aid of every sort except high tariffs, subsidies to private transportation lines, and below-cost postage rates for newspapers and magazines. Even from these quarters the protests had a perfunctory quality. Lanham of Georgia struck the expected Confederate note: "When an effort is made to bribe my state and the South with school construction money to accept the mixing of the races in our schools, I cannot vote for [it]. . . ." Republican Bruce Alger of Texas sounded the inevitable tocsin about "socialism." And John Henderson, Ohio Republican, was almost but not quite too pained to speak: "Federal aid to education . . . is a distasteful subject. . . . Education is a matter of local concern and local control." Clare Hoffman, a McKinley vintage conservative with a waspish manner and predictable reactions, expounded on what "our forefathers did when they needed a schoolhouse"—they took their axes and bucksaws, if they were lucky enough to have any, and went into the woods and built it. And he reminded a forgetful House that "Lincoln did not have any Federal aid . . . in getting an education."

It was not until the House, still sitting as the Committee of the Whole, threw the floor open to amendments that the real trouble began. It came, after a flurry of minor proposals, from three sources, all of which, whatever their purpose, played directly into the hands of those who wanted no bill at all.

The first of these was Mr. Powell's expected attempt to rule out Federal money for new schools in states that failed to comply with the decisions of the Supreme Court. The New York Congressman had warned his Committee colleagues that he would introduce his amendment, and although specific suggestions had been made to him for ways to achieve his purpose without hurting the school-construction bill, he could not agree. One of these alternative ways was to get a commitment from the Administration that, as an executive policy, it would allot no Federal funds to segregated school districts. And this Powell had tried. As early as February, he made public a letter from President Eisenhower's administrative assistant, Bryce N. Harlow, stating flatly that the Administration would *not* withhold funds from segregated schools unless told to do so by Congress. That, said Powell, made his amendment "mandatory." Amplifying its stand, the Administration, again through Harlow, advised a group of inquiring Democratic Congressmen on March 7 that "The Federal judiciary, not the Executive branch, is to determine how compliance with the Supreme Court mandate is to be brought about and what constitutes compliance in good faith." "So," said Adam Clayton Powell, "I have exhausted every possible avenue trying to find someone . . . who would speak the word so that I would be sure that my amendments were not vitally necessary."

There were in fact several to "speak the word," and in other years Powell himself was to do so. Rising to answer him, Richard Bolling of Missouri read a letter from former President Truman opposing the amendment, and William L. Dawson of Illinois, like Powell a Negro, made an eloquent plea for putting the need of *all* children, white and Negro alike, above the futile effort to include the ban in a bill which could only be doomed by it. From the outside the NEA argued that the amendment would "serve no useful purpose" and "would not hasten the integration of a single school system." Americans for Democratic Action took a similar stand, and President Meany of the AFL-CIO criticized the amendment as "unnecessary in view of the Supreme Court decision barring expenditures for segregated schools."

Some of the Southerners, in a melancholy way, likewise thought the amendment unnecessary and wondered why Powell wasted the energy. Whether or not it was adopted, said Colmer of Mississippi, was "not material"; the objective would be reached sooner or later through administrative action or the courts. "The states maintaining segregation in their public schools are going to be taxed to build schools in other states without receiving any of their tax money back" for their own. But the Colmers, now fearful about all school bills, were shrewed enough to know that if the amendment was adopted, their fellow Southerners would vote solidly against the bill itself, whereas some might otherwise be fooled into going along. Further, the amendment would all but guarantee a fatal filibuster in the Senate. This accounted for the fact that when the members passed down the center aisle between the tellers, to be counted for or against the Powell amendment, more than a few Southern Congressmen were to be seen lolling in their seats or standing in the back of the chamber. Naturally they could not vote *for* a proposition so abominable in character, but it was tactically smart not to vote against it. The amendment passed, 164 to 116, and the United Press sent out a news story that began:

> The House all but scuttled hopes for Federal school aid when it voted tentatively to deny help to southern States which refused to abolish racial segregation in their public schools. . . . The bill faces its biggest hurdle in the Senate. Southern Senators, already angered by the High Court's decision, would be in a strong position to try to kill it off during the last-minute drive for adjournment.

Early in the debate Graham Barden, who as Committee chairman was automatically floor leader for the bill, took the unique course of resigning his general's commission at the climax of the battle. Whether it was the Powell amendment or just a long-simmering dissatisfaction, he announced that, being now opposed to the bill, he would step down and let Kelley manage it. The suspicions of his Committee colleagues over the months and years as to the depth of their chairman's conviction appeared to have been justified. At any rate Barden now felt free to move an amendment to reduce the authority of the Commissioner of Education, lest he "foul up the situation," and tried to choke off debate. In the end he would vote solemnly against the whole bill.

No sooner was the Powell amendment embodied in the measure than a quirk of the House machinery enabled Representative Gwinn of New York to knock it right out again and to come close to sinking the bill itself in the process. An emphatically conservative Republican with no use for any Federal aid to the schools, Gwinn suddenly moved to substitute for Title I of the bill a scheme of his own. Instead of the Federal government's apportioning aid by flat grants or on the basis of need, each state would get back one percent of the Federal taxes collected within its borders. With this rebate it could presumably solve its own school problems.

Floor leaders were caught off guard by the Gwinn maneuver, evidently regarding it as no more than the diversionary mischief of an extremist. In the brief debate that followed, opponents of the amendment invoked the name of Robert A. Taft, who had recently denounced the same proposal in the Senate on the ground that once the States were conceded a property right to taxes collected within their boundaries, the entire Federal financial system would collapse. Driving home the inequity of the scheme, Mrs. Green of Oregon sarcastically offered Gwinn a "Biblical sanction" for his amendment from the

Gospel according to St. Matthew: "For unto everyone that hath shall be given, and he shall have abundance; but from him that hath not shall be taken away even that which he hath."

But argument on amendments in the Committee of the Whole are held to five minutes for each side, and there was not enough time to round up absentees. With no more than half the members on hand, the Gwinn proposal squeaked through on a teller vote, 122 to 120. Under the House rules a successful amendment that replaces a title, or section, of a bill with an entirely new one automatically wipes out all other amendments previously made to that title, which meant in this case that Gwinn's amendment had the incidental effect of wiping out Powell's. Now the bill pleased neither the ardent integrationists, who wanted the Powell safeguard for its own sake, nor the segregationists, who wanted it for the damage it might do the bill on the final vote. What is more, it pleased neither the all-out champions of aid to the public schools, since it would distribute the most funds where least needed, nor the Administration, whose emphasis was all on limited aid to needy states only.

In the parliamentary wrangle that ensued, Powell reintroduced his amendment to the bill as a new Title IV, and McConnell, the Committee's ranking Republican, offered an amendment which would have replaced both the Gwinn and Kelley plans with the original Hobby proposal. McConnell's attempt was turned back with some bitterness, but not before its proponents made it clear that "The Kelley bill never was the Administration program; it is not the Administration program now." What was left of the little bipartisan amity with which the bill had left the committee was now thoroughly dissipated.

The new Powell amendment, which had been hurriedly scribbled out, quickly ran into roadblocks of a frivolous sort. It had referred to "provisions" of the Supreme Court, and several Southerners pointed out that the Court handed down "decisions," not "provisions"; after which they most politely refused to go along with a unanimous consent agreement for the necessary verbal change. At length Representative Roosevelt of California succeeded in getting a favorable vote on this grave bit of editing, and a little later the Powell amendment itself was restored to the bill by a vote of 177 to 123.

Then the Committee of the Whole rose, as it were, and gave way to the House of Representatives. Francis Walter, who had presided as Committee chairman, formally reported its work to the Speaker, who was now back on the dais. It was then proper to demand roll-call votes on the amendments adopted by the Committee of the Whole, and such demands were heard in connection with the Gwinn and Powell contributions. By this time, of course, notice of a record vote had brought absent members trooping back into the chamber, and the tallies took a different turn.

The Gwinn proposal was turned down, 168 to 250. If they expected the bill to pass, Southerners should logically have been against this amendment, since it was clearly, even crudely, designed to benefit the richer states of the North. Yet a solid bloc of fifty-eight Southerners voted for it, presumably on the theory that the worse the amendments, the less chance for the bill. The revived Powell amendment sailed through, 225 to 192, with 148 Republicans making up the bulk of the winning vote. But, significantly, many of them were shortly to vote against the bill itself. The third roll call was on a last-minute move by McConnell to send the entire bill back to the Committee, with instructions to substitute the Administration's original Hobby formula for Title I. Those who wanted the bill defeated now saw no need for this particular evasion; with the Powell amendment safely included, the bill would be defeated anyway. The move to recommit was accordingly beaten, 158 to 262.

Nothing was left now but the final record vote on the bill

itself, and as the names rolled out it became apparent that it would not survive the adverse Republican vote plus that of the disaffected Southerners. The count against it was 224 to 194. Breaking down the result, students of the game found two significant facts: Of the 119 Republicans who voted against the bill, 96 had only minutes before voted *for* the Powell amendment. That they were moved in this high proportion solely by a sudden concern for civil rights is improbable, especially since many of them were from districts with negligible Negro populations, in states like Nebraska, Iowa, and Oregon. The greater likelihood is that they were anticipating the second significant fact: With two exceptions, every one of the 105 Democratic votes *against* the bill came from Representatives of Southern or border states, whose acceptance of the Powell amendment would have meant political suicide. According to James L. McCaskill, the NEA's legislative expert, something like half of these same Southerners had been for a school construction bill all along, until the introduction of the Powell amendment. The estimate may be high, but the fact is that a switch by only sixteen of them would have carried the bill through the House. A year later success for the perennial supporters of Federal aid was to come even closer, only to elude them even more frustratingly.

Stricken in the Enacting Clause—1957

In the fall of 1956 Adlai Stevenson called Federal aid to the schools "one of the major issues of the campaign" between himself and President Eisenhower, adding that "people everywhere" were "indignant about the failures of the Eisenhower Administration in this field." The President, he said, had "sat by while Republican Congressmen first supported an antisegregation rider to the bill and then voted against the bill itself." To all of which the President loftily replied that an "opposition-controlled Congress" had killed his bill but that he would willingly take responsibility for "not allowing" an "unacceptable Democratic bill." Allowing for campaign niceties, the fact remains that both nominees must have been convinced that public opinion was still in favor of getting Federal money into the schools—so much so that party weakness on the subject was considered a political disability.

When the Eighty-fifth Congress convened, President Eisenhower, returned to office, was accordingly bound to make another attempt. His proposal, made in a special message to Congress on January 28, was not appreciably different from his effort of the year before. It was offered as an "emergency measure," designed only to "stimulate" construction of schools by state and local efforts. The emphasis again was on need and the degree of effort put forth by the respective states to meet it. The issue would be debated, Eisenhower hoped, "on its own merits, uncomplicated by provisions dealing with the complex problems of integration."

Had the President stood firmly by all these positions, right or wrong, he would have had a bill to sign and an achievement to celebrate. In his Economic Report for the year he was still firm—"No proposal for enlarging our national resources is more important than for Federal assistance in overcoming the critical shortage of schoolrooms." But from that level his comments during the battle were to range, as we shall see, through a bewildering series of comments down to the tired remark, following the bill's defeat: "I am getting to the point where I can't be too enthusiastic about something that I think is likely to fasten a sort of albatross, another one, around the neck of the Federal government." Hardly the spirit needed to rouse a body already gripped by the power of negative thinking.

As in 1956, the Senate decided to let the House take the lead, seeing little point in proceeding until that chamber should

move further than it had yet been able to go. Into the House
hopper had gone the usual quota of school-aid bills, and the
Committee on Labor and Education, faced with some kind
of decision, knew exactly what was needed: more hearings.
These extended over a period of five weeks, and the only significant change from all the earlier ones lay in the shifting emphasis of the opposition. Critics of Federal aid to the schools
spent less time and energy warning of the dangers of Federal
control and more on the alleged ability of states and localities
to do the job for themselves. The classroom shortage, they
said, had gradually declined and there was no longer need
for Federal action, if there ever had been.

In particular the United States Chamber of Commerce took
this tack, in direct contradiction to the testimony of Marion
B. Folsom, who had succeeded Mrs. Hobby as the Administration's Secretary of Health, Welfare and Education. Folsom
had estimated the shortage at 159,000 classrooms, with an
additional 59,000 to 65,000 needed every year for increased
enrollment and replacement. Since the current construction
rate was about 69,000, he pointed out, very little headway was
being made by the states toward reducing the chronic deficit.
The Secretary charged the Chamber with "seriously misleading and inaccurate statements" in its statistical argument, and
the Chamber countered with the charge that in obtaining its
own figures of need, the Office of Education had used "coercive
tactics" in order to produce exaggerated results.

The Chamber position was backed principally by the Investment Bankers Association, the American Farm Bureau,
the National Association of Manufacturers, and the American
Legion, none of which now conceded the need for any general Federal aid program. On the other side, seventeen organizations, headed by the NEA, sent a joint letter to Folsom
registering surprise "that the Chamber of Commerce has
launched a misleading and inaccurate propaganda campaign."

And Americans for Democratic Action found the Administration's own program far short of what was needed—in Edward D. Hollander's words, "a penny-pinching, half-starved bill, with the marks of the budget wringer still fresh upon it."

In the circumstances, Subcommittee Chairman Cleveland Bailey announced, "We're going to have to have a compromise to get a bill approved." The compromise reached by the full committee was, financially, something between the earlier Kelley bill, itself a compromise, and the Administration program. It was, in short, a more conservative bill than the preceding year's, although a majority of the Committee accepted the classroom figures of the government as being "as accurate as any that may be obtained."

The Committee likewise followed the Administration's lead in rejecting an antisegregation amendment, but ominously for the bill an attempt to include it had been made and would therefore be made again on the floor. This time the amendment was not offered, in committee, by Mr. Powell. On the contrary, he warned against attaching it to the bill at that point, for fear of giving opponents a pretext to defeat the measure before it could even get to the floor. It remained for the amendment to be offered, in Powell's absence, by Stuyvesant Wainwright, of New York, an Eisenhower Republican from Long Island who made no pretense of favoring Federal aid to the schools.

The bill was approved by the Committee on May 9, by a vote of 20 to 9, six Republicans taking the trouble to sign a minority report to the effect that the shortage was "nowhere near as serious" as it was represented. Among these, notably, were Wainwright and William H. Ayres of Ohio, both of whom were to play major roles on the floor.

Between May 28, when the bill was reported out, and July 23, when it came up for debate on the floor, Administration Republicans gave increasingly the impression of men alarmed at the prospect of getting the compromise they had supposedly endorsed. As late as April the President had told the NEA, in a speech, that the country's "educational plant is not ample to cope with the enormous burden of present and future enrollments. Therefore, it is my firm belief that there should be Federal help to provide stimulus to correct an emergency situation. . . . Federal help in building schools will not mean Federal control." And just before the Committee bill was reported out in May, Representative McConnell, its ranking Republican member, told his colleagues of assurances by the President that their compromise bill had his "full support." But by June Representative Frelinghuysen, likewise a Republican, reported a correspondence with the White House in which Mr. Eisenhower's ardor for the bill had cooled in proportion to its prospects for passage. The exchange, said Frelinghuysen, who really wanted a bill, was "somewhat disappointing."

Soon afterward, however, an aide to Secretary Folsom announced that there was "no question that the Administration would support" the bill as it was and would not press for amendments. On July 22 Folsom himself called a press conference to answer criticisms of the bill and to observe that "The President and I are deeply concerned that the people understand the facts in this matter." But the next day, with the bill scheduled to go to the floor, the winds from Pennsylvania Avenue blew cool again. Returning from the White House, Republican leader Joseph W. Martin reported the President "not entirely satisfied" with the measure, though probably ready to accept it. A delegation from education associations and parent-teacher groups, in town for the climactic fight, tried all day to get a more spirited word from the President but were brushed off without sympathy by Sherman Adams, his assistant and a power in his own right. Between conservative advisers like Adams and liberals like Folsom, who reportedly had been reprimanded for in effect committing Eisenhower to the bill's support, the gap was wide and the President uncomfortable. Charitably, Democratic Representative George McGovern of South Dakota explained on the floor that the President "likes everybody so well that he embraces with equal good humor all possible sides of issues."

Past the opening salvos of rhetoric, the House quickly got down to cases. Republican Stuyvesant Wainwright brought in his antisegregation amendment, as expected. Few Congressmen from urban areas could afford to vote against it, and as before, some gladly voted for it in the knowledge that it must poison the bill for Southern and border Democrats. Wearily, Representative Kelley pleaded, "Most of us remember what happened last year when the so called Powell amendment was adopted. It was a good excuse for many members to vote against the bill, and I fear the same thing will happen today." It did not have a chance to. What happened was less expected and, for the bill's supporters, more devastating.

With the House sitting as the Committee of the Whole, the Wainwright amendment was passed, easily enough, by a vote of 136 to 105, with many Southern members, as in 1956, absenting themselves from the test. In fact if only half their absentees had turned out for the vote, they could have defeated the amendment then and there. But it was shrewder to leave it in, the better to beat the bill itself on the final vote—or at worst to doom it to a filibuster in the Senate.

As matters turned out, however, this stale maneuver was not necessary. Standing in the wings with another amendment was Representative Ayres, the Ohio Republican who, like Wainwright, had voted against the bill in committee. Ayres now offered the House as a substitute the bill originally asked for by President Eisenhower the year before, basically the proposal drawn up by Mrs. Hobby in 1955. "This is the bill that the President is really for," he announced. "This is the bill he supported in the last session. This is the bill, in my judgment, after having talked with him at breakfast in the White House, his heart is really in." Representative Halleck, a party stalwart, rose in congratulation. "I commend the gentleman from Ohio for offering this substitute. It is President Eisenhower's program. I voted for it last year and I shall support the substitute this year."

Perhaps he would have, but he did not get the chance. In the light of his vote it is safe to say he did not want the chance. The Republican leaders apparently expected supporters of the more liberal Kelley bill, along with opponents of all Federal aid, to fight off the Ayres amendment, and they were completely caught off guard by what happened. In a scene of considerable confusion a group of Democratic stalwarts in the long fight for a school bill—chiefly Frank Thompson of New Jersey, Richard Bolling of Missouri, Stewart Udall of Arizona, and Lee Metcalf of Montana—agreed to yield "all the way." Knowing their own bill doomed, they were ready, to the apparent chagrin of the Republican leaders, to compromise for the sake of getting some legislation at last, however limited. With the liberal Democrats thus capitulating to the Administration and the Southerners suddenly shorn of the segregation issue—the Wainwright amendment would be automatically deleted by the Ayres substitute—it looked as though nothing could stop the House from finally passing a general aid-to-education bill.

But the House was equal to the occasion. For men on the point of winning the day, Republican House leaders seemed strangely disturbed until saved from victory by the quick thinking of Howard W. Smith, Democrat of Virginia. Don Irwin, writing in the New York *Herald Tribune,* a Republican newspaper, reported the scene:

> Behind the rail in the rear of the House chamber, Representative Leslie C. Arends (R., Ill.) the minority whip, was

seen in anxious conversation with Representative Charles A. Halleck (R., Ind.), normally an Administration stalwart. Representative Halleck left the floor. Less than five minutes later, Representative Smith moved to strike the enacting clause.

Chairman of the powerful Rules Committee, and one of the shrewdest parliamentarians on the Hill, Smith was an inveterate foe of any extension of Federal involvement, particularly in newfangled schemes for promoting the general welfare. Concerning aid to the schools his position was simple:

> This is an innovation. We are starting off on an entirely new road, a road that the American people, from the founding of the Republic, have said that we should never follow. That is to permit the control of our public education to go out of the hands of the local people. . . . They have to come with their hats in their hands, they have to comply with all the regulations, they have to grovel before a Federal bureaucrat in order to get the money back for their states which their states sent up here with the blood of taxation year after year in increasing amounts.

The weapon Smith now brought up against this dire danger was one of the harshest in the parliamentary arsenal. A motion to strike out the enacting clause, as indicated in earlier chapters, is literally an attempt to remove from the measure the "Be it enacted" phrase, without which formula it cannot become law. In practice it is a device for unexpectedly shutting off debate, and it allows members to vote against a bill without appearing on the record to have opposed it in substance.

Since a motion to strike the enacting clause is "preferential" under the rules, discussion of the pending Ayres amendment had to stop at once. Debate on the Smith motion was then limited to one five-minute speech in favor and one against. Now the liberal Democrats, as taken aback as the Republicans had been a few minutes before by their willingness to accept the Eisenhower formula, tried vainly to turn the tide. Udall pleaded against the Smith maneuver:

> Finally, after two years thrashing around on this thing we have reached an agreement on Ayres' amendment. We on this side have decided to go all the way with the President, cross every "t" and dot every "i" and go down the line with precisely what the President wants. We can join hands with you. . . . We can pass a school bill today.

To no avail. Here was a chance to kill the persistent measure quickly and, as Smith invited, "be through with this rather futile debate." On a teller vote Smith's motion carried 153 to 126. It was a rare opportunity for opponents of the bill, open and secret alike, to strike at it without having to bear the onus of a vote against virtue.

But there was still a thin chance. Having got through the House as Committee of the Whole, the motion to strike the enacting clause would still have to be passed by the House itself—and by an embarrassing roll-call vote. Before that could happen word from the President might again reverse the battle. All day, in fact, rumors had been buzzing that the White House was about to issue a statement, the Associated Press carrying the report as late as one o'clock in the afternoon. Now that the pro-aid Democrats had completely committed themselves to the President's version of the bill, he would surely rally his own forces on the Hill to upset the teller vote and pass the bill. Even without a public statement, a telephone call to Martin or Halleck would do the trick.

The word did not come. In the official silence of the Administration, the President's party leaders in the House went their separate and indifferent ways. On a roll-call vote the Smith motion squeezed through, this time by 208 votes to 203. Counted in the majority were 111 Republicans, all voting in effect to deny themselves the opportunity to vote for what would be their own President's bill. Halleck, who less than an hour before had declared himself in favor of the Ayres substitute, was among those who voted for the Smith motion to keep it from ever coming to a vote.

So it was that at the moment the House appeared ready to give President Eisenhower the very program he had requested, to pass at long last a bill to put Federal money into the building of public schools, the parliamentary advance was again wiped out—this time in a flash flood that left witnesses dazed and gasping. A switch of three votes would have made the difference, and a pro-Eisenhower newspaper was to observe scathingly, "If the President could not have summoned a half-dozen Republican votes to his cause on an issue which he considers vital, he has indeed reached a low level of influence on Congress."

When it was all over, the President expressed "great disappointment." At a press conference six days later a reporter questioned him about the last-minute willingness of the Democrats to accept his own proposal by way of the Ayres amendment. "I never heard that, Mr. Folliard," he replied. "If that is true, why, you are telling me something I never heard." And he went on to remark that he was not one to high-pressure the Congress, which was true. "I don't get up and make statements every twenty minutes. I don't think that is good business." But he would have another bill ready, he said, for the next session of Congress—a dazzling prospect of more hearings, more charts and statistics, more debate, and more maneuvering.

7

Domain of Howard W. Smith [1]

Exaggerating only mildly, one might say that the United States has, unique among the governments of the world, a tricameral legislature. Besides the Senate and House of Representatives, which are prescribed in the Constitution, it has the House Committee on Rules, which is not. A bill *can*, of course, become a law with the blessing of only the first two, but an important or controversial measure that comes to flower over the objection of the Rules Committee is in recent dec-

[1] Logically this discussion of the Rules Committee should have preceded the chapters on the floor, since by its very nature the Committee normally makes its contribution to the legislative process *before* a bill reaches the stage of open debate. This is not always the case, however, as we shall see, and, even more important for the purposes of this book, the destruction of bills calling for Federal aid to the schools has by chance followed a chronological pattern that makes this arrangement more plausible: They were killed in committee in the 1940s, on the floor in the 1950s, and by the Rules Committee in the early 1960s.

ades exceedingly rare and its sponsors extremely astute, not to say lucky.

Unlike the two better known chambers, the Rules Committee meets in a cubbyhole of a room in the Capitol, most of the time in executive session, behind closed doors. The members sit around a long oval table that runs the length of the room, with a few additional seats provided at one end to accommodate witnesses and, at occasional open hearings, a small complement of reporters. Considering all the legislation that has been buried there, it is not an impressive crypt.

At the head of the table sits Howard Worth Smith, a tight-lipped man with rimless glasses, now pushing eighty. Gentleman farmer, banker, and one-time Virginia circuit judge, Smith has only in recent years abandoned the wing collar that seemed so pointedly to fix him in time and place. The witnesses who appear before him are usually other Congressmen, come to plead for a resolution, or "rule," which will allow their bill to come to the floor of the House for a vote. Often they have been through this procedure before, sometimes repeatedly over the years, and their tempers are none the better for the experience. A committee chairman whose group may have spent weeks carefully working out the terms of a compromise bill after many earlier weeks of hearings, is inclined to resent having to repeat all his old arguments before a jury that may know little about the subject and care less—a jury, moreover, that is not obliged to account to anyone for its arbitrary decision to grant the rule, to refuse it, or simply to sit on the matter until the Potomac runs dry.

The result is that the Rules Committee has without question put more of a strain on Congressional courtesy than any other institution on Capitol Hill. In one of his excellent "Letters of a Congressman," the late Clem Miller of California noted that the Rules hearings he had attended had been "extremely rancorous, with argument largely in clichés and stereotypes, expressive of attitudes rather than of much effort at fact-find-ing." Representative Bailey of West Virginia often complained of its "undemocratic and un-American gag-rule procedure." Metcalf of Montana, now a Senator, talked bitterly of "six willful men,"—six was enough to block legislation then; now it takes eight—who had "arrogated to themselves the power of determining what bills the House shall or shall not consider."

The rancor goes back at least as far as the mid-1930's, when the newly established anti-Roosevelt coalition of Republicans and conservative Southern Democrats first discovered the pos-sibilities of the Rules Committee as a trap for New Deal legis-lation. Old hands on the Hill still remember when Eugene Cox, an excitable member from Georgia, swung at the nose of Chairman Adolph Sabath, receiving two well-aimed, though feeble, punches from that venerable New Dealer in return. It is true that Cox observed a few minutes later in the best Congressional manner, "I have a genuine affection for Adolph. He's a fine old man." And Sabath, according to observers, re-ciprocated with, "Gene is really a capable gentleman." But the bitterness was unmistakable for all that, and the atmosphere that produced it has only soured further with age.

Such are the powers assumed by the Rules Committee that the tension is not hard to understand. Elected on the same basis and with the same constitutional limitations as any other Congressmen, this handful of Representatives have vested themselves with an authority that might be reasonable only if Rules were in fact the duly constituted steering committee of the majority party, properly charged with enacting the pro-gram by which that party would stay in power or give way to the opposition. It has never been entrusted with any such function, of course; yet it goes its independent way, respon-sible neither to the Speaker, the President, nor anyone else—sometimes not even to its own chairman.

Basically the power of the Rules Committee derives from

the fact that of the ten thousand bills that are introduced each session, not even the hundreds that are reported out by the standing committees can be sensibly dealt with in a strictly numerical order. To take an admittedly extreme case, a resolution calling for a declaration of war could hardly wait six or seven months for its turn on the calendar while the House ploughed ahead with changes in the postal rates, bills to exterminate starlings in the District of Columbia, and the like. Somewhere the power had to be vested to give a measure a special rule for immediate action, which is to say, to fix priorities.

For years this was one of the functions of the Speaker, who also ran the Rules Committee. Desperate over the chaos that had long prevailed in the chamber, the House shortly before the Civil War made the Speaker a member of Rules, which then proceeded, thanks to a series of rulings by his successors, to assume, quite gradually, its current attitude of sovereignty. From deciding simply on a logical order for bills to go to the floor, it took to deciding, for substantive reasons, which should go at all and which be quietly interred. Then, bit by bit, it took to advising the standing committees to fit their measures to the Rules Committee's legislative views if they wanted them cleared for action. It fixed the time limits for debate on each measure and often laid down the law as to which sections might be amended, if any.

The combination of these powers with those the Speaker already had—principally to grant or withhold recognition on the floor and to appoint the standing committees—grew so overwhelming that Speakers like Thomas B. Reed and Joseph Cannon came closer to being autocrats than any American President has yet dared to be.

Like most autocrats, they seemed unable to gauge the resentment they produced. "I have been through it all," Cannon observed with more smugness than syntax. "Rain don't always

follow the thunder." But in 1910 the rains came, in the form
of a revolt led by the brash and fiercely independent young
Congressman, George W. Norris. And when the skies had
cleared, Cannonism was washed out. The power of the Speaker
was diluted, though not altogether dissipated. He would no
longer appoint committees, but his influence in their composition was to remain considerable, and he would no longer be
a member of the Rules Committee.

The revolution was well aimed, but like so many other
revolutions, it got rid of old wrongs only to nurture new ones.
The powers that had been the Speaker's by virtue of his position in Rules were now those of the Committee alone. And
where the Speaker had at least to be elected by the House,
the chairman of the Committee would achieve and hold his
position solely by longevity and be answerable to no one.

For years the powers left in the Rules Committee lay un-
exploited. Successive chairmen conceived of the group's role
simply as that of a traffic manager, charged with keeping bills
moving in a logical flow, according to priorities set up by the
party leadership. The notion had seemingly entered no one's
head that the hierarchy of the House or the House as a whole
would allow this one committee to sit in arbitrary judgment
on the work of the standing legislative committees, blocking
their bills at its pleasure. And there is no reason to think they
would have as long as the Democrats in Congress were still a
reasonable facsimile of a party.

They were at least a facsimile until the advent of Franklin
D. Roosevelt. The chances of a split between the Southern
and Northern varieties had been minimized before that by the
fact that Northern Democrats in Congress were numerically
meager and ideologically not different enough from their
Southern colleagues to make life together uncomfortable. But
by the mid-1930s things had changed. The Northern cities and
the West had sent sizable delegations of liberal Democrats to

Congress, labor unions were on the march, and the New Deal, once the country had been pulled out of the depths of depression, was beginning to appall the more conservative Southerners. In the Rules Committee Joseph W. Martin of Massachusetts, soon to become Republican leader, and Eugene Cox, the battling Georgian, were old friends who found it increasingly fruitful to explore ways of combating the flood of daring legislation. Cox's "opposition to the New Deal was much more ingrown than mine," Martin wrote years later in his autobiography, "and he was ready to fight to any lengths to keep further power out of the hands of Franklin Roosevelt." It was not even necessary, he added, "to offer any *quid pro quo* for conservative Southern support. It was simply a matter of finding issues on which we saw alike." When President Roosevelt committed the political folly of attempting to "purge" some of these Democrats in the election of 1937, including Judge Smith, the affair grew warmer on both sides. With the principals shyly denying the very existence of a coalition, the alliance ripened and has long since been accepted as one of the major facts of Congressional life.

What looked like a first-rate reform in 1910 had a quarter century later turned into a legislative nightmare. The bitterness engendered under Roosevelt continued under Truman and was in no small degree responsible for his campaign denunciations of the "No Good, Do-Nothing Eightieth Congress." Since that was a Republican Congress, the Rules Committee was chaired for the session by its ranking GOP member, Leo J. Allen of Illinois. So sublime was its self-confidence by then, and so sweeping the field of expertness it claimed, that it thought nothing of rejecting a universal military training program sought by the President, the Defense Department, and the House Armed Services Committee. After prolonged hearings and deliberation, Armed Services had given the measure a favorable report and appealed to Rules for what should have been mechanical clearance to the floor. But Chairman Allen, rightly or wrongly, frowned on the whole idea, so it got no further than the door of the Rules Committee. Former Supreme Court Justice Owen J. Roberts, who had had a hand in planning the program, was shocked into a public statement on this "travesty of the American system of representative government." In the same session the all-knowing Rules Committee barred the way to a labor bill, amendments to the Social Security Act, and a civil-rights bill.

If President Eisenhower fared somewhat better at the Committee's hands, it was only because he sent to the Hill legislation less likely, on the whole, to trouble the dreams of Leo Allen in 1953–1954, or of Howard Smith, who succeeded to the Chairmanship in 1955. Actually, Rules sometimes helped Eisenhower, though there again its procedures would hardly have recommended themselves to champions of sound government. There was the notable occasion, for example, in 1953, when Mr. Allen flatly informed Representative Daniel A. Reed that his tax-reduction bill, disliked by Eisenhower but approved by Reed's powerful Ways and Means Committee, would never emerge from the Rules mausoleum. Almost apoplectic, the aged New York Republican rose on the floor to inquire, "What have I done in the last thirty-four years that I should be subjected to this treatment here?" And when, in retaliation, he blocked a tax-extension bill sorely needed by the budget-minded Administration, the Rules Committee sent to the floor its own extension bill, crudely bypassing Ways and Means altogether.

Concerned that Allen had overstepped the tolerable limits, House leaders settled the immediate issue by placating Reed with a compromise. But the Committee was riding high and not so easily checked. In the same Congress, the House had passed a Hawaiian statehood bill by a vote of two to one, and the Senate had approved a measure to confer statehood on

Hawaii and Alaska as well. To settle the difference between the two bills the House had either to vote unanimously to send its bill to a conference committee of both chambers, a virtual impossibility, or get a resolution to the same end from the Rules Committee. For denying this pure formality, this minor mechanism for carrying out the will of the House, no possible argument could exist except the argument of naked power. But the Rules Committee, or at least its coalition members, numbering six, were not in the mood for new states. The resolution accordingly went into the dead file, and for five years more the stars in the flag remained at forty-eight.

In this period of developing power, the Rules Committee learned that, besides killing bills outright, it could force substantive changes in them as a price for letting them reach the floor. As early as 1946, in fact, it went so far in this direction as to substitute the Case labor bill in its entirety for a measure reported out by the House Labor Committee. It forced the sponsors of wage-hour legislation to accept such extensive changes that Christian A. Herter, then a Republican Representative from Massachusetts, was moved to declare, "If that is not a unsurpation of power, entirely improper in this House, I do not know what is." Protesting to a committee on the reorganization of Congress, Representative Eberharter of Pennsylvania reflected some of this same sense of outrage:

> Many a chairman of a legislative committee which had considered legislation for months and months was ordered by the Committee on Rules to change the provisions of legislation before a rule would be granted. That was a denial of the purposes of setting up legislative committees. It was a distortion of the purpose for which the Committee on Rules was set up. It was a denial of the right of the members to vote upon legislation.

But it was not until Howard Smith assumed the chairmanship, in 1955, that the Rules Committee hit its full stride.

Judge Smith may have given up his wing collar but not the
political and social attitudes that went with it. In the words
of a Congressional colleague, he is "an 1810-vintage thinker, a
Jeffersonian in his own estimation but one who is willing to
adopt any means to his ends." Even his political foes concede
him a Virginian graciousness of manner and a tactical wiz-
ardry in the ways of the House; but they see him sharing
rather less of the Jefferson philosophy than of the Hamiltonian
view that the people can't be trusted to know what is good
for them. In a single television program in 1961 he managed
to go on record against minimum wage laws, civil rights legislation, Federal aid to the schools, Federally supported medical
care for the aged, and continuation of foreign aid. While no
one can properly question his right to hold and promote these
views, or any other, in Congress or out, reasonable doubts
may be entertained as to his right to impose them, by way of
the Rules Committee, on Congress and on the country. Yet
on this same television program Smith was asked point-blank:
"The Rules Committee has been said to work for conservatism
and to have stopped liberal legislation—that is true, is it not?"
And the Judge, unabashed, replied: "I think that is a fair
criticism."

The record will bear him out. Since Smith's accession, the
Rules Committee has killed or for years delayed action on a
variety of legislation that the Judge personally regards as "socialistic." In his first year as chairman he completely suspended
hearings on a civil rights bill when a Committee quorum once
failed to show up for a session. Usually this is regarded as a
mere technicality, and in any case it had no bearing on future
sessions, but for Smith it was an opportunity to be rid of an
obnoxious measure. He alone could convene the committee,
and as he put it, "I'm not interested in calling a meeting."
Under his chairmanship Rules managed to string the statehood
bills along for several more sessions, but in the end they

eluded it as "privileged" measures which did not strictly require its blessing. Four times it pigeonholed resolutions, already passed by the Senate, to authorize a Congressional study of the Presidential succession. It squelched fair trade bills and bills to tighten Congressional control over the Central Intelligence Agency. And it tried hard to wreck a bill to bring Federal aid to depressed sections of the country, which managed to escape its clutches and pass, only to run into a Presidential veto.

It was in the Eighty-seventh Congress, however, that Mr. Smith's Rules Committee had perhaps its finest hour. In that Congress it managed to do in no fewer than twenty-three pieces of important legislation already approved by standing committees, including bills to assist the country's failing systems of mass transportation, to establish a youth conservation corps, and, inevitably, to pump still-needed Federal money into the public schools.

The revolution of 1910 had come full circle, and most Congressional scholars acknowledged it. Rules had been encouraged in 1910 for the purpose of making House proceedings more democratic, said Representative Metcalf, and it had "now become as arbitrary and arrogant as was old Speaker Joe Cannon." But Judge Smith has always seemed to feel that the 350,000 people of the Eighth District of Virginia, a collection of twenty rural counties whose closest approach to a metropolis is Charlottesville, had somehow vested him with powers beyond those of the run of Representatives.[2] No doubt he was

---

[2] In *The Deadlock of Democracy*, James MacGregor Burns points out that Smith started out as Representative from the Arlington–Alexandria district; but when that suburban area began filling up with politically unreliable immigrants from across the Potomac, the powerful Byrd machine had the Virginia legislature carve out for him a new and overwhelmingly rural district, which would send him back to Washington term after term with no need for anxiety.

right in saying, as he often did, that "My people did not elect me to Congress to be a traffic cop," but there is no more reason to believe that they elected him to sit in solitary judgment on all matters, animal, vegetable, and mineral, that might come before that body. The Washington *Post* aptly summed it up: "The spectacle of the policies of a Democratic President, who also is the leader of the Democratic Party, being obstructed by a Democratic Congressman, acting for the Democratic majority of a committee that is the agent of a Democratic House, is one to amaze Americans and confound foreign observers."

Political institutions with far-reaching powers rarely flourish for long, however, without making a case, articulated or not, for their existence. And to this general proposition the House Rules Committee is no exception. The arguments may not be unanswerable—indeed, they have been readily and repeatedly answered—but they exist and are very much a part of the picture. Briefly, the case for leaving the Rules Committee in the fullness of its present powers runs like this:

1. The standing legislative committees have something of the character of special interest groups, with Agriculture generally composed of Representatives from farm districts, Interior heavily weighted with Westerners, the Veterans' Committee with veterans, and so forth. Somewhere in Congress there has to be an agency that takes the over-all view, that can reconcile conflicting claims and fix priorities. The Rules Committee is strategically placed to do so. The alternative would be to return this function to the Speaker, which would only revive the evils of "Cannonism" and undo the Revolution of 1910.

2. The Rules Committee can keep an eye on the entire *spending* program of Congress, whereas the standing committees necessarily think only in terms of what comes before them.

3. The power of Rules to manage the flow of legislation is

far from absolute. A discharge petition signed by 218 members will force out any bill the House wishes. A measure can also be brought to the floor under a suspension of the rules any time two-thirds of the members want to debate it. Or it can be brought up under the curious device known as "Calendar Wednesday." Theoretically, on two Wednesdays of the month the chairman of a standing committee, whose alphabetical turn has come, may invoke the privilege of calling up one of his bills that may have been bottled up in Rules. Almost invariably at some point on Tuesday afternoon the Speaker makes the hurried and routine pronouncement: "Without objection, Calendar Wednesday will be dispensed with," and rarely does anyone rise to make the single objection necessary to cause trouble. But the opportunity is there if an aggrieved chairman wants to make use of it.

All of these arguments for Rules have been advanced many times. At one point when changes were contemplated, Representative Rankin of Mississippi expressed the fear that tampering with the Committee would expose the country to "a barrage of unwholesome, unnecessary, unreasonable and unstable legislation." Clarence Brown of Ohio, a Republican member of Rules, warned similarly of a flood of "wild, wasteful, socialistic" legislation. And even Rules Chairman Sabath, stout New Dealer though he was, contended that "We have some lopsided committees who report bills in the interest of . . . their own districts, states or sections. . . ." Smith himself has plausibly contended that it is better to have all the members of the Rules Committee, "coming from all sections of the country," make such controlling decisions, than to leave them to one man as they are left to the Majority Leader in the Senate.

To all these arguments, naturally, there are counterarguments, to wit:

1. The work of defining and sharpening legislation is entrusted to the standing committees, but the overall view, the

balancing of interests, must be left to the House itself. That means, in effect, to the majority party of the House, expressed through its policy committee, its chosen officers, or its entire Congressional caucus. Certainly no eight members out of a body of 435, clinging to their posts solely by seniority and responsible to no one, should be entrusted with this vast power. Even with the utmost objectivity, which nobody claims for the Rules Committee, it could not sensibly sit in judgment on every bill reported by every legislative committee on every subject from the price of aspirin to lunar exploration.

2. It is the function of the Committee on Appropriations, not the Rules Committee, to correlate the spending programs of Congress and serve as watchdog of the Treasury.

3. Not one of the methods currently available for circumventing the Rules Committee, so that the House may "work its will," is politically or mechanically practical. The weaknesses of the discharge petition, discussed in Chapter I, are so great that its use is an extreme rarity. There is a prejudice against using it that crosses party and ideological lines; not only because it is a clumsy way to bring legislation to the floor but because it carries with it a fear of reprisal from the bypassed committee. Even many of those who argue for the *status quo* on the ground that bills *can* get to the floor without approval by the Rules Committee refuse on principle to employ the alternative of the discharge petition. A device for "legislative chaos," some have called it, and others derisively characterize any attempted use of it as a failure of majority leadership. There may well be an element of self-serving and partisanship in these attacks, but Richard Bolling, a liberal Democrat and a member of Rules, is no doubt right when he says that the method "is actually opposed by a great many perfectly honest members of Congress. . . . It's very difficult to get a discharge petition signed up because

of this reluctance on the part of some liberals as well as conservatives."

The notion that the Rules Committee can be circumvented by introducing a bill under "suspension of the rules" is a minor joke. A motion of this sort requires a two-thirds vote, debate on the bill is limited to forty minutes, and no amendments from the floor are permitted. A measure that can meet those requirements might be important, but it could hardly be controversial—not even controversial enough for the Rules Committee to hold it up in the first place.

Those who would outflank the Rules Committee are therefore left with Calendar Wednesday, which is like bypassing the improbable for the implausible. A chairman might wait a dozen or more weeks before his committee would be called on the slow, frequently skipped roll call for Calender Wednesday, which was created as a sop to would-be reformers of Congress and appreciated as such. "A homeopathic dose of nothingness," Norris called it. When a bill does reach the floor by this route, it must, under the rules, be debated and resolved the same day, which is an open invitation to all the dilatory maneuvers in the book. One of the extremely rare instances of success on Calendar Wednesday was afforded by the depressed-areas bill of 1960, and the experience, in spite of wide sentiment for the measure, showed clearly why this method is not often attempted. The proceedings went something like this:

> Shortly after session convenes at noon, Majority Leader is informed that usual procedure to dispense with Calendar Wednesday will be objected to. Speaker accordingly orders call of committees.

> Opponent of bill suggests absence of quorum, which is verified by count. Three separate roll calls are then read, as members stroll in and out, each call taking thirty minutes.

Daily Journal for preceding day is read in full, objectors refusing customary unanimous consent to dispense with that ceremony.

Absence of quorum again suggested, this time requiring four roll calls, before *Journal* reading is finished.

Journal interrupted for third quorum call, most opponents of bill having left House precisely to make quorum difficult to achieve. Three more roll calls.

Shortly past five o'clock bill itself is called up and opposition leader asks for roll call to decide whether House should consider it. Loses request but not before clerk is obliged to read entire bill, thirty-six pages.

Substitute bill offered by opponents, likewise read in entirety. Following other substitutes and amendments, measure itself is debated for two hours.

Bill brought to vote, 9:30 P.M., after ten hours, nine of them pure waste.

On this rare occasion a Calendar Wednesday bill was passed, but as a rule obstructionist tricks have their intended effect. With the evening wearing on and the substance of a bill yet to be debated, its proponents, unable to hold their ranks, usually give up and go back to hoping for a regulation green light from the Rules Committee. They are lucky, perhaps, to have lasted until evening, because at any point in the long day when their majority was momentarily lacking, an opponent could have brought in a sudden and undebatable motion to adjourn. Once such a motion was carried, Calendar Wednesday would be gone—and so would their bill.

With all the cogent arguments against the Rules Committee, why hasn't the House done something to free itself? Fifteen years ago the Eighty-first Congress did in fact trim the committee's power. After twenty-one days of fruitlessly requesting action, it decided, a standing committee chairman could bypass Rules and get a decision directly from the House itself. The change seemed to work well, bringing out several major bills that had aged to an antique yellow in the Committee's files. Why, then, did the Eighty-second Congress, a scant two years later, repeal the 21-day rule and go back to the discredited system?

The answer lies in the great unwritten, only confidentially spoken, argument for keeping intact the power of the Rules Committee. It would be stretching to regard it as a moral argument, but for all too many Representatives it is a compelling one. On the loftier of its two levels, the theory is that Rules protects the members from having to yield to pressure from their districts for legislation that they know is ill-advised. "Take so-called fair trade legislation," a particularly frank Congressman explains. "The price-fixing it calls for has been opposed by economists, by the antitrust division of the Justice Department, and by two Administrations. It is contrary to the whole antitrust concept, and is really opposed by a majority of Representatives. Yet if it ever got to the floor it would go through like greased lightning," because to vote against it would be to vote against the "little guy," the corner grocer and the independent druggist, who, with all their supporters, have considerable retaliatory power at the polls. A Midwestern Republican was "willing to bet that ninety percent of the House is glad they're bottling up the fair trade bill."

In this use of the Rules Committee there is obviously more evasiveness than courage, but it is at worst the grateful tribute that principle pays to prudence. On a lower level is a Congressman's deliberate use of the Committee as a device for enabling him to talk out of both sides of his mouth. Clarence Brown, long a Republican power in Rules, tells of members who denounce the Committee to their constituents for holding up a bill and then tell him in private how grateful they are for being taken off the spot. Sometimes, according to Brown, they go even further: "I've had the experience of having people come to me and ask me: 'Please, whatever you do, hold the bill in until after my primaries are over, because either way I vote on it, I will be in trouble at home.' And then I get letters from his home areas in which they say: 'Now, we know what you people are doing . . . because our own Congressman has written and told us that it was the damnable Rules Committee that was blocking consideration of the bill.'" Members have been known to go so far as to sign a discharge petition so that they can tell constituents all about their great effort to force a bill out of Rules, and then, before it is too late, request the Clerk of the House to strike their names from the petition, just to make sure it doesn't succeed.

Such maneuvers are accepted by many Congressmen as legitimate moves in the game—"You can't be a statesman if you're not re-elected"—but certainly not by all of them. Some are genuinely concerned about the moral aspects of using a Congressional agency in this shabby way, and others are disturbed as well by the Committee's inevitable misuse of such power. A Representative ought not to require "protection" from his constituents—if he isn't up to voting on the issues, says Holifield of California, he needs a "wet nurse"—and he cannot expect to have such protection except at a price. John V. Lindsay of New York fears that the system enables the Rules Committee to "cudgel people into line," on penalty of being denied the intervention of Rules on some future occasion when they want it. Perhaps Representative Hoffman of Michigan was too sweeping when he observed that "Every single member of this House loves and approves of the action of the Committee on Rules when they protect us from going on record on some bill that is not sound or where we do not want to be on record." To Lindsay, as to others, "It is a bad concept to have an institution set up as insurance against the people." The trouble is, there are not enough others.

8

No Rules for Schools

The Russians fired Sputnik I on October 4, 1957, stealing a considerable march on the United States. Unable to find a better explanation in a hurry, many Americans surmised that their school system was at fault: Johnny not only couldn't read, he couldn't send a two-stage rocket to outer space. In something of this frame of mind, it took Congress not quite a year to pass from shock to indignation to legislation.

What emerged on Capitol Hill in the fall of 1958 was still far from broad-gauge Federal action. The National Defense Education Act was rather a "crash program" to help the nation's schools catch up with the Russian, which up to then had been thought by millions of Americans to be concentrating exclusively on the simpler aspects of Newtonian mechanics, outmoded farm technology, and Marxist-Leninist gibberish.

Among the provisions of the Act was one calling for Federal grants to the states for programs that would specifically

157

strengthen the teaching of science, mathematics, and modern languages in the public elementary and secondary schools. To supporters of Federal aid it looked as though precedent had been set with a vengeance. To extremists it looked like so grave a breach in the dike against Federal "interference" in education that the fanatical Senator Jenner moved an amendment specifically excluding his state of Indiana from any of the bill's benefits—an amendment which the Senate jocularly whooped through on a voice vote.[1] The mood of the moment was irresistible. Education was the new panacea, and teachers were suddenly "our first line of defense," enjoying momentarily a reverence normally reserved for mothers and the FBI. "History will smile sardonically," said Robert M. Hutchins, "at the spectacle of this great country getting interested, slightly and temporarily, in education only because of the technical achievements of Russia, and then being able to act as a nation only by assimilating education to the cold war and calling an education bill a defense act."

Only slightly less skeptical, Senator McNamara of Michigan expressed anxious hope and continuing doubt:

> With an assist from Sputnik, the Administration is at last taking education seriously. Unlike Venus, rising full-blown from a shell, scientists do not develop full-blown from our seats of learning. . . . My heartfelt hope is that Congress will provide the facilities so sorely needed. . . . Then we won't need a crash program to cope with each new crisis that comes up. *We'll be ready for them as they come.*

To this very end Representative Metcalf and Senator Murray, both of Montana, introduced companion bills calling for a Federal outlay to the States of $25 for each school-age child. The grant, to be used for either school construction or teach-

---

[1] In the House, Indiana representatives, facing election campaigns, saw to it that the unconstitutional damage was undone, as Senator Jenner knew perfectly well they would.

ers' salaries, as the individual state thought best, was to be
stepped up annually for four years, when the maximum provision would be $100 per pupil. To qualify, a state would have
to put forth a financial effort according to a formula that took
relative income and other factors into account, and safeguards
were, as usual, included to prevent the poking of Federal fin-
gers into matters of curriculum.

The Defense Education Act, however, had served as a ca-
tharsis, exhausting Congressional energy on the subject for the
session, and the Murray-Metcalf effort was in consequence
to receive a quick brush-off. After intermittent hearings a subcommittee favorably reported it to the House Committee on
Education and Labor, and there it stopped. Far from being
receptive to anything so ambitious, the full committee could
not even bring itself to act on the reintroduced bill of 1957,
so repeatedly blessed by the Eisenhower Administration. The
President, evidently past his peak of enthusiasm on the subject, now studiously said nothing, a circumstance that persuaded every Republican on the committee to line up against
it. Those who had formerly supported the measure and were
plainly embarrassed under the grilling of the bill's Democratic
defenders, feebly suggested that the thing "needed more study."
Confronted then with transcripts of a thousand pages of testimony left over from the year before, they were driven to explain, as one of them did with striking unoriginality, that "times
have changed." In any event the best the proponents could get
was a 15-15 tie, which was not quite good enough for action.
Joining the 13 Republicans were Landrum of Georgia and,
no longer surprisingly, Chairman Graham Barden.

All this was to prove merely preliminary byplay, however,
a curtain raiser to the climactic spasms of 1959, 1960, and
1961. Adapting to the numerical facts in the case that expressive subtitle to Lewis Carroll's "Hunting of the Snark," these
might best be characterized as "An Agony in Three Fits."

Fit the First—1959

In the euphoric glow of the mid-term elections, Northern Democrats in the new Eighty-sixth Congress thought the time for Federal aid to the schools had struck at long last. So sweeping had been the victory that the new proportions in the House would give them numerical superiority over the Republican-Southern coalition, and they were happily interpreting the people's mandate to include a demand for more and better schools. Rep. Frank Thompson of New Jersey, a leader in the perennial wars for a thoroughgoing school bill, thought "the chances for its passage better than ever before." And to judge from the flood of bills on the subject, scores of other Congressmen must have agreed. Sixty to seventy such measures were introduced in the opening weeks, and one Senate bill alone carried thirty sponsors.

Of all these proposals, attention soon centered on three. A House subcommittee on education devoted itself to a revival of the Murray-Metcalf bill of 1958. The Senate education subcommittee focused on the same bill for a time and then on a substitute brought in by Senator McNamara for school construction only. And the Administration, finally abandoning the pretense of wanting direct grants of any sort, put forward a scheme to help needy school districts amortize their construction bonds—a "legislative monstrosity," the irate Senator Murray called it, which "should properly be called the Bankers and Bureaucrats Bonanza Act of 1959."

After fourteen days of inevitable hearings (590 pages and a wholly predictable cast) the House subcommittee approved the Murray-Metcalf bill (H. R. 22) by a 4-to-2, strictly partisan, vote. It then went to the full committee, which, it should now be noted, had undergone considerable change since Graham Barden's heyday.

The North Carolinian was still in charge and, like any other standing committee chairman, he had power, but he no longer ran the group with a high hand. After several years of mounting resentment, Committee members in 1955 had staged as much of a rebellion as ever occurs in these Congressional compartments charged with high-voltage courtesy. Led by Stewart Udall, later to become Secretary of the Interior but then a freshman of remarkable brashness, a majority confronted Barden with a demand for a set of rules similar to those already prevailing on several of the more enlightened committees. Senior members were not much interested in such reforms—regular meetings, with or without the chairman, freedom of subcommittees from the chairman's domination, and the like—but, as Udall observed much later, others *were*, including the newer Republicans as well as the rebellious Democrats. In any case, rather than risk an open defeat, Barden turned around and presented the panel with a set of rules of his own, which by coincidence he had been preparing and which by another coincidence represented most of what they wanted.

Udall could not have succeeded to the extent he did if Speaker Rayburn and the Democratic leadership had not throughout the Fifties built up the committee's liberal contingent at the expense of a membership that formerly tended to take its cues from the National Association of Manufacturers. Among the generally Fair Deal-ish additions, besides Udall himself, were Carl Elliott of Alabama, Lee Metcalf of Montana, James Roosevelt of California, Frank Thompson of New Jersey, and Edith Green of Oregon. The Democratic sweep in 1958, plus some committee departures, made way for three more liberals in the Eighty-sixth Congress—John Brademas of Indiana, Robert N. Giaimo of Connecticut, and James O'Hara of Michigan.

Where a few years ago Barden and the coalition would scornfully have rejected the subcommittee's endorsement of

so bold a bill as Metcalf's, they were now outflanked and
lacked the numerical strength to defeat it. It was passed, 18 to
12, two of the Democrats voting with the opposition, but not
before it had been considerably diluted. Instead of a permanent support plan, the committee contemplated only a four-
year period of assistance, and financially it scaled down the
amount of assistance by 60 percent. The recommended bill
still gave the states a choice of spending the funds on building
or on teachers' salaries, but the limitations imposed were a
concession to what were believed, no doubt correctly, to be
the political realities. If anything, the committee's majority
were not "realistic" enough. The Administration's early doubts
about Federal aid, both as a potential drain on the budget and
as a dangerous bit of centralization, had gradually deepened
into such distaste that a more substantial measure would
clearly have been headed for a veto. As it was, every Republican on the committee signed a minority report that called the
bill "an ominous piece of legislation" and talked of its "far-
reaching and deleterious effect upon our free society." What
was worse, reintroduction of the teachers' salary provision once
more aroused the anxieties of Catholic Church leaders; they
had been willing to go along quietly with Federal appropriations for public school construction, but they feared, with reason, the prospect of competing for teachers in a rising-salary
market.

On the other side of the Capitol the Senate had been going
through its own rituals. Majority Leader Johnson, like Rayburn in the House, saw school construction as the farthest
advance that could reasonably be expected and used his considerable powers to keep the salary question out of the picture. As a result, the Murray-Metcalf approach was quickly
shelved by the Subcommittee on Education, and McNamara's
School Construction Assistance Act (S. 8) was reported in its

stead. McNamara himself preferred the stronger bill (S. 2) as "the most adequate solution to the nation's educational problems," but he conceded that "opposition to S. 2, from many quarters, was of such a nature that passage would have been difficult, if not impossible."

The McNamara bill slid through the Committee by a vote of 12 to 2, Senator Goldwater of Arizona alone filing a minority report. But just as the Metcalf bill in the House had stirred up Catholic misgivings, the Senate bill now drew ominous rumblings from the National Education Association, which was in no mood to return to a "half-loaf" emergency construction bill. At its summer convention the teachers had, in fact, adopted a resolution rejecting "as being unsound and unwise national policy all proposals to compromise the basic principles embodied in the Murray-Metcalf bill, eliminating either teachers' salaries or school construction."

As had happened so often in the past, such bothersome questions were disposed of by time and Congressional machinery. It was September 11 before S. 8 emerged from committee, and it hung harmlessly on the Calendar until the session ended, four days later. H. R. 22, on the other hand, had gone to the Rules Committee as long before as June; but with the Speaker no more in favor of it than that redoubtable committee itself, the bill was allowed to rest there in peace and the dubious hope of resurrection in the session to come.

No sooner was Congress adjourned than the House Education subcommittee, chaired by Rep. Cleveland Bailey of West Virginia, sat down to a serious attempt at working out a new bill for introduction in 1960. A spirit of compromise prevailed, Bailey being determined that no bill would be pushed in 1960 unless he had advance assurance of President Eisenhower's willingness to sign it into law. This appeared to mean that the best that could be had was a long-term measure providing help in paying off bonded indebtedness, but nobody could say. The members laid the problem of devising a compromise in the lap of the subcommittee staff and went home for Christmas.

Fit the Second—1960

However mellow the House champions of Federal aid may have felt in the holiday season, their Senate counterparts returned to the capital filled with the joy of battle. Following an abortive attempt by Republican Senators Javits and Cooper to interest President Eisenhower in a compromise bill of their own—he had "reservations," they reported—Senate leaders plucked S. 8 off the Calendar early in February and sent it to the floor, a maneuver open to them by virtue of the fact that this was still the same Congress. Almost immediately Senator Clark moved an amendment that would have doubled the size of the grants, extended the program indefinitely into the future, and included teachers' salaries. So far had sentiment in the Senate advanced that even this drastic modification achieved a 44-to-44 vote, and the tie had to be broken, in favor of the nays, by Vice President Nixon. A slightly milder amendment, retaining the two-year limit but likewise providing for salaries, was then passed, 54 to 35. Shrewdly foreseeing that this would revive opposition from Catholic Church circles, Senator Morse tried vainly to sweeten the bill with a two-year program of loans to private schools, for construction only; and Senator Dirksen made the inevitable attempt to substitute once more the Administration's stark program of help in paying off the bondholders, a proposal that won the President a resounding repudiation, 25 to 61.

The amended S. 8 was passed on February 4 by a vote of 51 to 34. "This is a very proud moment for the Senate," Majority Leader Johnson remarked by way of observing the occasion. "In two working days we have passed one of the most far-reaching and most constructive pieces of proposed legislation in which it has been my privilege to participate since I have been a member of this body." But President Eisenhower's reaction had an ominous ring: "I do not believe the Federal Government ought to be in the position of paying a local official. If we're going into that, we'll have to find out every councilman and every teacher and every other person that's a public official of any kind, or public servant, and try to figure out what his right salary is. And I think—I can't imagine anything worse for the Federal Government to be in."

Since the bill left the question of salaries completely to the state governments, which presumably had figured out pay scales for their public servants, the President's comment was wide of the mark. But if his logic was murky, his attitude was clear. House supporters of Federal aid, having taken this into account, along with the effect on their Republican colleagues, had in fact written off H. R. 22, their own counterpart of the Senate bill. A little stunned, in fact, by the Senate's militancy, Frank Thompson felt called upon to explain: "In the House it is perfectly evident that we cannot possibly hope to get H. R. 22 out of the Rules Committee. Our subcommittee, headed by Representative Cleveland M. Bailey, has been working this past week attempting to draft a moderate, a reasonable bill limited to school construction."

By past standards H. R. 10128 was indeed a moderate measure. It was for construction only; it called for matching state funds, and as an option to grants it provided for commitments to aid in the paying off of bond issues. The hope, as far as the militants went, was to get any sort of bill through the Committee and through Rules—and then to strengthen it on the floor. Beating off amendments of all sorts, with this objective in mind, a healthy majority of 19 to 11 voted to report the bill out, Democrats Barden and Landrum again joining the opposition, and Republican Frelinghuysen joining the supporters.

It was March 25 when the Committee sent the bill to Rules, and when nothing was heard of it by the middle of May it looked as though it would share a funeral vault with H. R. 22. It so happened, however, that earlier in the year the rarely successful device of Calendar Wednesday had been used to pass the Area Redevelopment bill, striking the Rules Committee with shock waves of dismay. As a result, sponsors of school legislation were less resigned than they might have been, and the Rules Committee, by contrast, less self-assured than usual. Taking advantage of Chairman Barden's absence from a Committee meeting on May 12, Representatives Thompson, Udall, and Brademas pried out instructions that Rep. Bailey, Chairman of the subcommittee, was to bring up H. R. 10128 on the first Calendar Wednesday the Committee's name could be reached, probably May 18. But twenty-four hours before the deadline, according to the Washington *Post*, the mighty chairman of the Rules Committee yielded. He "made it known that he would hold a hearing on the education bill on Thursday morning (May 19) if plans for Calendar Wednesday were dropped."

Smith had first opposed releasing the bill even under threat. But he had reason to believe that, for once, the coalition that had blocked so much social legislation with a 6–6 tie would not prevail, and it would be better for the Committee to yield by its own decision than to give further encouragement to the use of Calendar Wednesday. The break in the coalition, momentary as it was, arose from the fact that Republican Representative Reece of Tennessee was under considerable fire from financially hard-pressed school people in his district, who were aware that Rules had blocked aid in 1959. They had exacted from Reece a pledge not to bottle up another school bill in 1960. The result was that on May 19 the Thompson bill got a rule to proceed to the floor. Debate, the rule said, was to be limited to four hours.

The bill was brought up on May 25, and Bailey immediately and hopefully made the point that "It is particularly written and tailored to receive House approval. The job that faces me and other proponents of the legislation is to see that it is not muddied up from the introduction of a lot of side issues." In this they were only partially successful. An attempt to substitute the Administration program was quickly rejected on a voice vote, and so was a complicated revision of the allocation formula. The one important amendment that was adopted was that old, so often fatal standby of Mr. Powell's. And once again the familiar pattern was repeated. In spite of pleas and the example of Thompson, Bailey, and Udall, Northern Democrats facing election campaigns went along with Powell, who cheerfully branded a vote against the amendment a vote against the Supreme Court and civil rights. Most Republicans who were opposed to the bill were only too happy to vote for the embarrassing amendment, and the Southerners, as before, ducked into the cloak rooms, the Speaker's lobby, and other places of asylum, trusting that without their indignant opposition the amendment would carry and then serve to kill the bill.

The amendment did carry, and 78 Republicans who supported it then turned around and, on final passage, voted against the entire bill as predicted—among them Minority Leader Halleck and Rep. Byrnes of Wisconsin, who was chairman of the Republican Policy Committee. If this was "the best proof" that the alleged coalition was responsible for inclusion of the amendment, as Thompson told his constituents a week or so later, it was a strategy that, at long last, failed. Such was the composition of the Eighty-sixth Congress that the combination of Republican and Southern Democratic strength was not quite up to the necessary follow-through. It lacked the votes to beat the bill, even with the usually fatal amendment included. For the first time in history the House passed a general aid-to-education bill, 206 to 189.

At long last, after a century of intermittent efforts, *both* Houses had now passed such bills in the same session. Among veterans of the movement hopes were at the peak, even though President Eisenhower was known to be sour by this time on any outright Federal grants for education, and especially to abhor the teachers' salaries provision in the Senate bill. After all, 1960 was an election year, and, for all his feelings in the matter, Eisenhower might well think it inadvisable to compromise the campaign chances of Mr. Nixon with a veto, particularly since both parties were about to include in their campaign platforms planks calling courageously for Federal support of the country's primary and secondary schools. When the House took its historic action on the 26th of May, it looked very much as though the long fight had come at least to the beginning of the end.

Yet, unbelievably and without any assist from Mr. Eisenhower, the legislation was stone dead before the end of June.

Elsewhere in this volume the mechanics have been described whereby a House bill that differs materially from its Senate counterpart may be sent to a conference committee for reconciliation. Such differences existed in this case, and Senate Majority Leader Johnson now made the formal request for a conference to iron them out, advising the Speaker that the Senate would be represented by Hill of Alabama, Murray of Montana, McNamara of Michigan, Yarborough of Texas, Case of New Jersey, and Javits of New York—all committed to the measure in principle—and Goldwater of Arizona for negative ballast. There was every reason to believe that the conference would have been successful, since the basis for compromise was clearly present. The Senate probably would have dropped the provision for salaries (which would have helped at the White House, too) and the House would probably have dropped the Powell amendment to placate the Southern Senators. As late as June 17, Vice President Nixon's office announced that he was working for a school bill and had met with Halleck and with White House representatives. According to his press secretary, Herbert G. Klein, Nixon thought there was "a good chance a school construction bill will come out of conference and be acceptable to the White House."

As a routine matter, unanimous consent for a conference was asked in the House, and almost as routinely Rep. Johansen, a Michigan Republican and opponent of all school-aid legislation, objected. This meant that the question would go, as a matter of course, to the Rules Committee for a conference rule. Nobody was perturbed because nobody dreamed that the Rules Committee, which had given the bill a green light *before* it reached the floor, would veto it *after* a House majority had voted in its favor.

Yet on June 22, meeting in executive session, the House Committee on Rules declined, by a 7 to 5 vote, to clear the approved measure for conference. Why did Trimble and Reece, who had voted to send the bill to the House in May, now vote against sending it to conference? Most observers assumed that Trimble, from Arkansas, could not politically afford to promote a bill containing the Powell antisegregation amendment. Reece, it was explained, having technically fulfilled his pledge to the teachers of his district, no longer felt obliged to vote against his extremely conservative convictions.

The more fundamental question was, who had charged the Rules Committee with the power to override legislation favored by both Houses of Congress, and what would be done about it? In any but the most literal sense, of course, no one had given the Rules Committee any such power. As for the balance of the question, from June 22 until Congress adjourned

on September 1, nothing at all was done about the great usur-
pation, and for obvious if insufficient reason. The year was
1960, and the magic word was "politics."

Everyone, it seemed, had a stake in letting Mr. Smith and
his colleagues get away with an act of arrogance unmatched
since the days when "Uncle Joe" Cannon rode the House of
Representatives bareback. In a large way, the Republicans
were grateful to be rescued from a choice between having
their President veto a popular measure in an election year and
having him sign it after he had all but sworn not to. For many
Democrats, on the other hand, the bill's failure would be grist
for the campaign mills. Nixon's expressed hope for a compromise exposed him to Thompson's gibe that "The Vice
President was completely repudiated by all of the Republicans
on the Rules Committee. This is a great victory for Charlie
Halleck, who has more influence here than Nixon does."

Militant advocates of aid to the schools may have been carried away in viewing it as a decisive campaign issue, and the
NEA, in particular, indulged the dream to the point of abandoning all efforts to force a compromise in 1960. At the very
start of the session it had warned that "If no satisfactory school
support bill embodying the principles of the Murray-Metcalf
bill is enacted in the next session of Congress, the Association
will endeavor to make this matter a major issue in the political campaigns of 1960 so that the American people may again
express their mandate for the enactment of such legislation in
1961." Aware that any agreement that would come out of a
conference committee would probably be at the expense of
teachers' salaries, the NEA thought it best to withdraw from
the field and lay plans for another battle.

Among the insiders, some had even more subtle reasons for
leaving bad enough alone. Five Democrats on the Rules Committee had voted to send the school bill to conference, but
in the long gap from June to September none of them made

a fight of it. "We were planning a full-scale attack on the power of the Committee," Bolling explained privately a few years later, "and we felt that the worse it looked, the better."

With everyone who might otherwise have had a mind to protest its arrogance happily pursuing his own will-o'-the-wisp, the Rules Committee followed to the end its blandly domineering way. From time to time pronouncements came from high places. Speaker Rayburn suggested that the Committee's action would be reversed. Vice President Nixon said he thought the bill "still has a chance" and that "it is not dead." But on August 24, at a closed meeting, would-be insurgents on the Committee were told bluntly by their chairman that there was no hope for this or any other social legislation, except the minimum-wage bill—take it or leave it. The following day Mr. Smith departed for his Virginia farm, announcing he had called his last meeting for the session. And on September 1 Congress adjourned, a week before a record-breaking 37,600,000 children returned to schools short of classrooms, classrooms short of teachers, and teachers short of money.

"The will of both House and Senate must yield to a little group of wilful men on the Rules Committee," said Rep. Thompson. And he added prophetically, "A concerted and determined effort must and will be made to reform the Rules Committee and its procedures, if the next Congress is Democratic."

Strange Interlude

Politically it was understandable that no one wished to force a showdown with Judge Smith on the eve of a national election. For both parties the sensible thing in such periods is to avoid quarrels, alienate no one unnecessarily, postpone all unpleasantness. But once the election was past, the President-elect knew that a collision was inevitable, that if a way was not found to rein in the Rules Committee, or at least break the coalition's grip on it, his program would scarcely reach the outposts of the Old Frontier, never mind the New. Being John F. Kennedy, formerly a member of the House of Representatives, he knew, too, that the impetus for any drive to curb the Committee could not come from the White House without alienating a large number of Congressmen. The move would have to be sparked by men on the Hill, and they would have to be committed not only for his sake but in their own right.

On this score the timing could hardly have been better. Smith's highhanded refusal to send the school bill to conference in the summer of 1960 had so incensed a large number of Representatives that on a single day toward the end of August a round dozen of them rose on the floor to denounce the Committee on Rules and demand reform. Foremost in the assault were members of a recently formed faction of House Democrats which called itself the Democratic Study Group. About a hundred strong and spearheaded by Metcalf of Montana, Holifield of California, Udall of Arizona, Thompson of New Jersey, Blatnik of Minnesota, and Roosevelt of California, the bloc was concerned not so much with formulating liberal policy as with coordinating efforts to put it into effect. By no means an extremist lot, they knew they would have to work through Speaker Rayburn and they had no desire to do otherwise.

Even two years before, so significant were the liberal gains in 1958, Rayburn had found himself giving the Study Group serious attention. But he was not yet willing then, on their advice, to press for institutional changes to curb the power of the Rules Committee. He much preferred, instead, to work with its members as individuals, to arrive at a personal understanding, in the immemorial way of Congressional politics. While he declined, therefore, to support a drive for restoring the 21-day rule, touched on in the preceding chapter, or even to reduce the number of signatures required for a discharge petition, he assured the liberal bloc that he would persuade the Committee on Rules to send to the floor all major legislation reported out by the standing committees of the Eighty-sixth Congress.

But "Mr. Sam"—fellow-Congressmen sometimes referred to him so, though not as generally as newsmen said they did— had signally failed to deliver. Largely the difficulty lay with changes in the Republican leadership. Ironically Rayburn had often had his way with the Rules Committee in the past by reaching an understanding not with Smith, but with Joseph W. Martin, his Republican counterpart. Through Martin he could often manage to pry a vote from a moderate Republican on Rules and so pragmatically get over the hump from time to time. But at the opening of the Eighty-sixth Congress House Republicans had replaced the easygoing Martin with the highly partisan, hard-driving Charles Halleck, in addition to which the two moderate Republicans on Rules had left the House. More and more the Speaker had found his overtures rebuffed.

Now, two years later, at the start of the Eighty-seventh Congress, a chagrined and irate Rayburn was in a mood for stronger action. Apart from his wounded sensibilities, he was genuinely concerned for the program of the new President, whom although he had earlier supported Lyndon Johnson, he had come to admire extremely. Even if this were not the case, circumstances would have dictated that as Democratic Speaker he would have to work closely with the first Democratic President in eight years. In any case, at a pre-inaugural session with Kennedy in Palm Beach on December 20, Rayburn promised the President-elect that all major items in his program would come to the floor, and he well knew that this could not be done without somehow shaking up the Committee on Rules.

His hope was to do this with the least offense to any segment of his party.

Members of the Democratic Study Group, meeting in Washington ten days later, largely agreed as to what they wanted done but avoided saying anything that would strike Rayburn as a premature decision, much less an ultimatum. What they wanted was simply the removal from the Rules Committee of William M. Colmer of Mississippi and his replacement with a Democrat acceptable to their bloc or at least to the House leadership.

Admittedly a temporary and *ad hominem* solution to a long-range institutional problem, this proposal for a purge as it quickly was called, had a certain compelling logic. Colmer had opposed his party's Presidential ticket in the 1960 campaign and therefore rated no consideration *as a Democrat* when the party drew up its slate of committee members. He had served the minority; let him look to the minority for an assignment and thereby serve as an example to other turncoats. Since the purge could be effected within the Democrat caucus, where Rayburn held the power, the House itself would not have to take action and the Republicans accordingly would have no say in the matter. The net effect would be that with a minimum of disruption the 6-to-6 tie that had so long paralyzed the Committee on Rules would be broken and the President's program assured at least of reaching the floor.

On New Year's Day the wily Virginian, heading both Rules and those Southern Democrats without whom the new President could not command a majority in the House, came on invitation to the office of the wily Texan, the symbol of Congressional power and party regularity. He was given the chance to accept, quickly and simply, the way out that Rayburn himself greatly preferred either to the dropping of Colmer or tampering with the House machinery. This was to have the membership of his Committee increased from twelve to fifteen.

The Democrats, being in control, would naturally fill two of
the new vacancies and the Republicans one. Just as naturally,
the two new Democrats would be party regulars, unlikely to
side with Smith and the Republicans in the business of the
committee. But Smith saw no reason to accept the implied loss
of control without doing battle, and he said so.

Having made a mild proposal, in good faith, Rayburn was
now in a position to threaten the dropping of Mr. Colmer,
which he did not relish but which he was certain conservatives in the House, and others as well, would relish even less.
The next day he let it be known that he would press for the
purge, and as he anticipated, the news was greeted with something like horror. If seniority could not guarantee Colmer's
spot on the Rules Committee, it could no longer protect anyone else's and the whole sacred order was threatened. Yet
clearly Rayburn had the power for such an internal party
maneuver, and with the Judge's Republican allies thus pre-
cluded from coming to his aid, the old Virginian could not hope
to prevail.

Rayburn let these facts sink in for a week, and there is no
doubt that they had a certain persuasive effect. Informally,
Smith lieutenants soon approached Rayburn lieutenants with
suggestions for an arrangement. The Judge might deign, just
for the sake of peace, to relinquish for good his Committee's
control over the sending of bills to conference, which had just
proved so disastrous. What was more, he might graciously
guarantee that *five* of the President's major bills would be allowed to come before the House. If these legates spoke with
authority, Smith was displaying a humility comparable to
Marie Antoinette's.

That they did speak with authority was confirmed a few
days later when Smith called at the Speaker's office to propose this very offer. But Rayburn, pressing his advantage,
scorned it, and when word got out that negotiations had failed,

Smith's following began to crumble. Carl Vinson of Georgia, second in seniority and prestige among the House Southerners, then stepped in to seek the best possible terms. And what better terms were there than Rayburn's original offer? To something like half of Smith's seventy-two followers the enlargement scheme now looked acceptable. It would make no institutional change, and since the House adopts rules at the start of each session, the proposal was in any case applicable only to the one Congress—they could fight for a return to the twelve-man committee when circumstances should again favor them. Rayburn was only too glad to oblige. On January 11 he told a news conference that he had decided, after all, to ask for expansion of the Committee as a "painless" way out, "a way to embarrass no one unless they want to be embarrassed." Moreover, to avoid alienating anyone, he would not even ask his party caucus to bind Democratic members to support the plan. He was confident.

Unlike the Colmer substitution, enlargement of the Rules Committee would require a vote of the entire House, and on this score Rayburn was taking a genuine risk. He would not only have to hold on to the Southern votes assured him by Vinson but win some of the moderate and liberal Republicans as well. Defeat on an internal issue of such magnitude would leave him little in prestige or authority and would make Howard Smith virtual ruler of the House.

On January 11 Rayburn's strategy looked like a good gamble, but it quickly appeared he was in trouble. The very next day the Republican Policy Committee declared against the Rayburn move, and wavering Republicans were allowed to dwell on the fact that committee slates for the new Congress had not yet been drawn up.

For two weeks the Smith-Halleck forces on the one side and the Rayburn forces on the other waged a subterranean struggle to pin down every last available vote. It became clear very

soon that Vinson had not succeeded in prying as many Southerners away from Smith as he had promised, or at least not
as decisively. Under a deluge of letters and telegrams inspired
by the National Association of Manufacturers, the American
Farm Bureau, and local Chambers of Commerce, some were
wobbling badly. On the other hand, labor and liberal lobbies
were putting the heat on for the Rayburn position, and king-
pins of the new Administration were none too shyly telephoning their sentiments to possible waverers on the Hill. Among
those so engaged were Vice President Johnson, Attorney General Kennedy, and former Rep. Udall, who had just been ele-
vated to Cabinet glory and whose intervention touched off
special displays of resentment. It was not until the day before
the issue was first scheduled to come to the floor that the new
President himself spoke up. Discreetly he repudiated any notion of infringing on a matter so clearly the province of the
House, but as "an interested citizen," he could not refrain from
hoping that all the members of that body, and not merely
those on the Rules Committee, would "have an opportunity
to vote themselves on the programs which we will present."

As the showdown approached, both sides knew from intensive polling by their lieutenants that the issue would be decided by less than ten votes, and both accordingly played for
time. Rayburn was able to use his position to postpone the
vote from the 25th to the 31st, an act gleefully trumpeted by
the opposition as a confession of weakness. Smith again offered
to let five bills through without question, aid to education
among them, but the Speaker demanded, instead, a guarantee
that any Administration bill he personally requested would
be cleared by Rules for debate on the floor. Smith refused with
the conscience-clearing statement common to statesmen on
the eve of war: "We who oppose the packing scheme have
made every offer we properly could to settle the controversy
amicably."

On the 31st of January the battle was joined. Debate was limited to one hour, and if no one in the galleries was dazzled by its brilliance, the debaters did manage to cover all the main points. Clarence Brown, by then the Rules Committee's ranking Republican, made the inevitable comparison to the "attempt of Franklin Delano Roosevelt to pack the Supreme Court," and it fell to another Republican, Thomas B. Curtis of Missouri, to make the retort obvious: It *was* packing, he agreed, but he considered it "a basic proposition that whichever party obtains the responsibility to organize the Congress should have the necessary power to meet that responsibility. . . . The principle is a sound principle, and I think in this instance we make a mistake as the Republican Party to oppose this basic proposal."

Speaking solemnly of his conscience and getting a jocular reaction, Judge Smith himself found it necessary to add that "Some of these gentlemen who are laughing maybe do not understand what a conscience is." Nevertheless, he repeated the generous offer he had already made to Rayburn, and noting the talk about his "going out and milking cows once or twice," he threw in the pledge that if his proposal were accepted there would be no "undue delay in any call that the leadership makes to hold hearings in the Committee on Rules." After which came the bald threat: "If the resolution is adopted I make no commitments." Smith was most effectively answered by Rep. Blatnik of Minnesota, who found the offer "an insult to the House and its Members." The sincerity with which it was made, Blatnik suggested, "only heightens the frightening picture of two men telling a nation that they will permit five bills to pass if they can reserve their right to kill off any others that do not meet with their approval."

Halleck slyly injected the appeal to the individual member's self-interest in preserving the Rules Committee as a protection against his constituents: "Certainly the Committee on Rules is not obligated to report to this floor every bill that comes before it; and as I look around I see Members who I am quite sure are thankful for that." The Speaker himself then descended from on high to make the simple point that "this House should be allowed on great measures to work its will, and it cannot work its will if the Committee on Rules is so constituted as not to allow the House to pass on those things." Tellingly he observed that "The gentleman from Virginia says that he is not going to report anything that violates his conscience and then winds up his talk on the floor by saying you have nothing to fear from the action of the Committee on Rules." Winding up the debate, Rep. Conte, a Massachusetts Republican, appropriately quoted Charlotte Gilman:

> If fifty men did all the work,
> And gave the price to five,
> And let those five make all the rules—
> You'd say the fifty men were fools,
> Unfit to be alive.

The Muse having had her moment, the clerk proceeded to call the roll. So close was the sentiment that two-thirds of the way through the roster the count was exactly even, according to Neil MacNeil, whose account of the entire battle in his book *Forge of Democracy* is by far the most detailed and illuminating in print. Before the call was over, however, the Rayburn forces had inched slightly ahead and at last squeaked through with a 217 to 212 victory. A switch of three votes would have won for Judge Smith. It was no surprise that the Speaker had the solid support of Northern and Western Democrats, of most of the border-state Democrats, and of one-third of the Southerners. What won for him was the vote of twenty-two Republicans, who, while unenthusiastic about the method chosen, were as convinced as the Administration Democrats that something had to be done to dissolve a dangerous concentration of power. And what helped decidedly was the fact that of the nineteen committee chairmen besides Smith, including some decided conservatives, fifteen voted with the Speaker rather than with the man who had assumed powers encroaching on their own.

For "Mr. Sam," coming so soon before his death, it was a gratifying triumph. As for the future of Federal aid to the schools, however, it might be appropriate to call on another poet:

> "But what good came of it at last?"
> Quoth little Peterkin.
> "Why, that I cannot tell," said he;
> "But 'twas a famous victory."

Fit the Third—1961

When the Eighty-eighth Congress settled down to work in January, 1961, the prospects for a Federal aid bill were fairer than they had ever been before. Graham Barden had departed from the Congress, leaving its Committee on Education and Labor in the hands of his chief opponent, the Reverend Adam Clayton Powell, who not only favored such legislation but was now openly pledged against endangering it with one of his antisegregation amendments. The Senate was, as always, receptive to the legislation. And in the enlarged Rules Committee the votes of Messrs. Smith and Colmer would no longer be decisive, the Democrats having added Carl Elliott of Alabama and B. F. Sisk of California, both in favor of Federal aid to the schools. Above all, the newly inaugurated President, going far beyond the generalities of his predecessor, had made Federal aid one of his major campaign planks. He specifically favored grants that might be used for teachers' salaries as well as the building of schools, and it was felt that if anyone could urge legislation satisfactory to opponents of aid to parochial schools without stirring up bitterness, it would be the country's first Catholic President.

Yet on this issue more than any other the first session of the Eighty-eighth Congress was to mount to a peak of frustration and then slowly peter out in anticlimax. Of all the fits in the agony, this one has been reported in greatest detail,[2] probably because it evoked the greatest degree of public interest at the time. But in the full mosaic it is not one of the more colorful or revealing tiles and will accordingly be treated here only at modest length.

On February 20, President Kennedy sent to Congress a special message on education in which he requested, so far as elementary and secondary schools went, a three-year program of grants for the construction of classrooms and for teachers' salaries. Seeming almost to ask for challenge, the message proceeded: "In accordance with the clear prohibition of the Constitution, no elementary or secondary school funds are allocated for constructing church schools or paying church school teachers' salaries. . . ."

The Administration bill was introduced in the House by Frank Thompson, a Catholic, and in the Senate by Wayne Morse, who though not Catholic had strongly favored Federal loans to private and parochial schools. It cannot be said, however, that the choice of sponsors succeeded, if that was the intention, in taking the edge off the Administration's sharp approach. On the bishops of the Church, including the five American cardinals, who attended the March 1 meeting of the Administrative Board of the National Catholic Welfare Conference, the effect was in no way visible. Following the session, Archbishop Karl J. Alter released a statement that cast a pall over the bill's supporters. If there was to be any Federal aid, the bishops began mildly enough, they were

[2] Most notably by Prof. H. Douglas Price of Syracuse University, whose excellent study, "Race, Religion, and the Rules Committee," is included in *The Uses of Power,* edited by Alan F. Westin, Harcourt, Brace & World, New York.

"deeply convinced that in justice Catholic school children should be given the right to participate." Specifically they asked an amendment permitting long-term, low-interest Federal loans to private schools, and they concluded with an all-or-nothing stand: "In the event that a Federal aid program is enacted which excludes children in private schools, these children will be the victims of discriminatory legislation. There will be no alternative but to oppose such discrimination."

Reaction to the bishops' statement was quick in coming and hardly more conciliatory. Nineteen prominent Protestant and Jewish clergymen and laymen immediately drew up a pronouncement that it would be "most unfortunate for a major church to press its own interests in a way that would threaten the strengthening of our basic educational system," a sentiment widely echoed by individuals and newspaper editorials.

But it was in Congress itself that the division was to bite deepest. Catholic members themselves were split, and in answer to a direct question by one of them, Msgr. Hochwalt made it plain that, for all the campaign it might wage, the hierarchy claimed no authority to dictate the position of Catholic Congressmen. "We would expect them to vote according to their consciences. Nobody is going to try to persuade them to vote against their better judgment." Thompson himself remained firmly committed to an aid bill for public schools only, and his fellow Catholics went their several ways. Senator Hart of Michigan favored loans for private schools in addition, but only if such an amendment would not block passage of the bill. Senator Mansfield of Montana was neutral on the subject, commenting to newsmen, with what a *Time* reporter described as a worried smile, "I'm just waiting for the bells of St. Mary's to peal." And, most important, House Majority Leader McCormack said flatly: "There is certainly no constitutional question involved in the Federal government making long-term loans at reasonable rates of interest for the construction or the renovation or the repair of private schools." As *Commonweal,* a Catholic lay magazine put it, "It should now be abundantly clear that this is one of the questions on which there is no single 'Catholic' position," to which it added its own view that the bill already introduced, without parochial school aid, "deserves all the support it can muster."

At his press conference on March 8 the President appeared to be modifying his all-out stand. The Court, he repeated, had in his opinion clearly outlawed direct grants to parochial schools, but "There is obviously room for debate about loans. . . . This has not been tested by the courts." He still did not think across-the-board loans to parochial schools would be found constitutional, but he was, not altogether happily, willing to let the matter be explored. All he asked was that Congress pass the Morse-Thompson bill *first,* leaving the question of loans to private schools to be brought up separately and, if necessary, given its day in court. So arose the question that was to plague supporters of aid in this particular Congress: Should there be one bill, incorporating grants to public schools and loans to private, or should the public school bill, uncluttered by Constitutional and religious doubts, be pushed first, leaving the parochial-school advocates to rest their hopes on a follow-up measure?

Throughout March and April strategy meetings were held on Capitol Hill, attended by Democratic Congressmen, emissaries of the President, and representatives of the Department of Health, Education and Welfare, now presided over by Abraham Ribicoff. Tentatively it was decided that the way out lay in extending the National Education Defense Act, which would be up for renewal the following year. Since NDEA already included provision for loans to private schools specifically for the better teaching of science, mathematics, and foreign languages, why not add a provision for the construction of classrooms in which these subjects would be taught?

Senate hearings—inevitable and lengthy—were presided over by Senator Morse, who by general agreement did a masterful and statesmanlike job. Sympathetic to the Catholic position but determined to get a bill through, he found candor the best diplomacy, as the following exchange with Monsignor Hochwalt suggests:

> *Msgr. Hochwalt:* I have a feeling that one measure would pass in this Congress, the Federal aid as such. I have a feeling that a second measure, which would provide for our schools, wouldn't have much of a chance. So I am being very frank with you.
>
> *Sen. Morse:* Monsignor, I perfectly understand your view on that matter and your position. I think I would be less than honest if I didn't say, if I were sitting in your position, I would be rather inclined to hold tenaciously to the point of view you just expressed.
>
> *Msgr. Hochwalt:* I am encouraged.
>
> *Sen. Morse:* We just have some differences in responsibilities. That is all. I have the responsibility of doing what I can to further the President's program. . . . It is my best judgment at the present time as chairman of this subcommittee that I best serve my President, I best serve the educational cause of this country so far as Federal aid is concerned, by doing my level best to get a public school Federal aid bill to education passed first, and then to give all my support to a loan bill as I did last year.

To skip lightly over the hearings—1,300-odd pages of them —the Morse view, supported by Thompson in the other chamber, prevailed and early in May S. 1021 was sent to the floor. It contained some complicated changes to weight the help in favor of the needier states—Senator Dirksen was moved to

wonder whether the formula would require "a course in quad-
ratics, least squares, the fourth dimension, a book of log-
arithms, and probably an engineer's slide rule." It included
provision for extending the program for aid to impacted areas,
a section hopefully counted on to swing wavering legislators
who might be uninspired by the vision of schools but not by
the physical presence of a gravy train.

What the bill did *not* contain was any reference to the
NDEA. Just before the opening of debate, on May 16, Majority Leader Mansfield left a last-minute strategy meeting that
included Senators Morse, Humphrey, and Metcalf, Secretary
Ribicoff, and Lawrence O'Brien, the President's liaison man
on the Hill, to make an announcement. No attempt, he said,
would be made to tie the NDEA renewal to S. 1021. Ribicoff
and O'Brien had made a final effort in this direction, but
Morse and Humphrey fought it off in the reasonable belief
that the combination would doom the measure in the House.
For the next few days Morse was to fight off, with equal de-
termination, no fewer than fifteen amendments, involving civil
rights, religious discrimination, economy, and Federal control.
In the end only one significant change was voted through—
Senator Prouty's amendment to allow grant money to be used
for maintenance and operation as well as construction and
salaries.

On May 25, the bill was passed by the comfortable margin
of 49 to 34. One after another, seven leaders of the Senate rose
to pay tribute to the distinction with which Morse had piloted
through the measure described by Senator Fulbright as "the
most important bill the Senate will handle at this session."

Meanwhile, hearings before Cleveland Bailey's subcommittee in the House had taken twelve days and filled a couple
of printed volumes with much the same testimony heard in
the Senate. In the committee procedure perhaps the high
point was Republican Representative Frelinghuysen's attempt

to bring in the tired old Powell amendment, only to have
Powell himself lead the fight against it. He was concerned, he
said, about the Russians putting an astronaut into space ahead
of his own country.

More significant and less hopeful developments in the House
were going on behind the scenes. There Majority Leader Mc-
Cormack, who got along none too well with the Kennedys
in Massachusetts politics, was insisting that aid to parochial
schools, via the NDEA, precede or accompany any general
aid legislation. To this end he had induced Rep. Zelenko,
a New York Democrat with a large Catholic constituency,
to introduce a bill combining the Administration's program
with outright grants to nonpublic schools for "special purpose" classrooms, where potential scientists, mathematicians,
and linguists would be trained for the national advantage.
Cardinal Spellman was known to have thought well of the
move, if he had not, as alleged, directly inspired it.

In spite of McCormack's efforts, the Education and Labor
Committee itself had little trouble reporting out the original
Thompson bill, with minor modifications, late in May. But
for weeks thereafter a feverish atmosphere closed in on the
House, stimulated by an intensive barrage of letters, telegrams,
and telephone calls on both sides of the parochial school
question. Church officials, as Msgr. Hochwalt had promised,
refrained from direct pressure on Catholic Congressmen, but
they saw no more reason than their opponents to refrain from
stimulating pressures back in the districts. *Newsweek* quoted
a representative of the National Catholic Welfare Conference
explaining the strategy: "Congressmen always vote their constituencies. What we do is stir up the constituencies."

By the hundreds of thousands, the messages poured in, especially following television and radio exhortations to "write
your Congressman." Parochial schoolchildren turned them out
in streams and so did those who fancied they could hear the

wall separating church and state crumbling before such threats as the Zelenko bill. Thousands of the letters and telegrams were identical, to be weighed rather than read, but they worried the members just the same. As one of them pointed out, "When the form letters are followed by intelligent individual letters, and when people from your district call you up or come to see you about a bill, then you damn well better pay attention."

The Thompson bill got to the Rules Committee while Powell's Education and Labor Committee was still pondering separate aid to the parochial schools by way of the NDEA. The obvious strategy for supporters of the public school measure was to press for clearance as quickly as possible, before the other bill could arrive and touch off a religious debate, and to this end Rep. Bolling moved to begin Rules Committee hearings in a week. By the same token the five Republicans, plus Smith and Colmer, favored delay, but they were now a seven-man minority on a fifteen-man committee.

What happened then was what no one had anticipated when the Rules Committee was being saved for democracy simply by having its membership increased. The two new members voted with Bolling and the Administration, according to plan, but two old reliables—James J. Delaney of New York and Thomas P. O'Neill of Massachusetts, who sided with McCormack in favor of parochial school aid—went over to Howard Smith and the Republicans. The Bolling move to speed ahead was beaten, 9 to 6, and everyone knew the vote meant more than mere delay. Ray Madden, like O'Neill and Delaney a Catholic but one who chose to stand by the Administration, mused sadly, "I never thought I'd see the day when Jim and Tip would join the coalition of Republicans and Dixiecrats. It's the strangest alliance I have witnessed in all my days in Congress."

Of course the test would not occur officially until the NDEA bill actually reached Rules and was voted on along with the public school bill and a third measure for aid to the colleges. But if Delaney's vote was not sufficiently ominous by itself, he privately made it clear that unless parochial school assistance was cleared along with the other two bills, he would vote "no, no, no."

Prodded by the White House, Powell's committee a week later, voted 19 to 11 to report out the NDEA extension, by then generally known as the "parochial school" bill, and in due course it came to Rules. To the horror of his old colleagues, Mr. Delaney quickly let it be known that he considered it highly inadequate, "just a little bit of a sop," and the rest was purely mechanical.

On July 18, Rep. Colmer suddenly moved to table all three bills. O'Neill then moved back to the Administration side, on the ground that he did not want to kill the college measure, but Delaney's vote was enough to give the old coalition the victory, 8 to 7. Before anyone could change his mind, Colmer made a *pro forma* motion for reconsideration, and Brown obliged with the expected motion to table Colmer's. This was passed by the same 8 to 7 vote, thus precluding later reconsideration under the rules, and the three bills were carefully stuffed into the pigeonhole that was waiting to receive them.

For those whose interest is morbid enough to extend to what might be called the "post-anticlimax," an effort *was* made to salvage something from the wreck. At the prompting of the President an exceedingly watered-down bill was routed to the floor by way of Calendar Wednesday, but the spirit had oozed out of the enterprise and no one expected anything to come of it. The Church was still opposed because such aid as the bill provided was for public schools only. The Republican Policy Committee, as well as individual party members, came out against it on the ground that it was "hastily conceived," which was undeniable. The NEA called it "a woefully inadequate compromise," and liberal Democrats like Humphrey described it as "a patchwork that would please no one."

In this high-spirited atmosphere the House had no trouble declining by a vote of 242 to 170, even to consider the remnants of what the President had called his "most important piece of domestic legislation." Like so very many school bills that had gone before, it went down to dusty death.

9

What It Would Take

If there is ever to be full-bodied, all-around, general-purpose Federal assistance to the elementary and secondary schools of the United States, it will more likely be generated by sheer need, translated into cries of pain from the taxpayers, than by the foresight and deliberation of Congress. That much the record of decades seems to have made clear.

Observers may differ as to whether the degree of need required to produce such action is imminent or even inevitable. In spite of polls, editorial support, and a great deal of generally intelligent lobbying, the demand is not yet articulate enough to elicit from the average Congressman the keen, automatic interest he would show in the potential choice of a belle from his district as the year's Apricot Queen. Yet to the eye of the innocent beholder the need itself, coolly viewed and apart from any of the attendant clamor, would seem to

190

be great enough to trouble any member of Congress even moderately attuned to the rumblings of the electorate.

Such a member need only take note of the feverishly spreading tendency of hard-pressed home owners and small businessmen to vote down their local school budgets and bond issues; to learn that at least two million schoolchildren are quartered in outmoded and hazardous buildings, and that close to one hundred thousand of the nation's schoolteachers do not meet the often modest standards fixed by their respective states. He need only discover that some 22 million adult Americans boast less than an eighth-grade education. It should impress him to be told by the Department of Health, Education and Welfare that to overcome the gap between the existing school system and an adequate one would require a minimal investment of *four billion dollars a year* beyond what it now receives; to observe, on top of this, not only that the school-age population has gone up every year since the war but that it goes up by a greater number in each succeeding year; and to realize that while the small property owner has been squeezed very nearly to the limits of his tolerance, the fifty states, collecting among them no more than a quarter of the nation's total revenues, are in no position to lighten the property owner's burden appreciably, much less to make up the evergrowing deficit. "They cannot do what has to be done in the next ten years, which at a conservative estimate is to raise the expenditure on education to $30 billion a year," according to Walter Lippmann. "Why not? Because the demands upon states and localities have caused them to tax and to borrow at rates which cannot be raised much further. . . . In the postwar years state and local tax revenues have tripled and their debt has quadrupled."

Possibly the case is still arguable, but if so, it need not be argued here. For what is more relevant than the actual degree of need is the fact that in the endless legislative rounds need itself has very rarely been the touchstone. Proposed legislation to aid the schools has been beaten over and over again not because the nation's school system was ever shown to be in admirable or even satisfactory shape, but because of wholly extraneous considerations like race and religion, or secondary ones like a vague fear of Federal control and simple-minded penny pinching.

Short of waiting, then, for a taxpayers' explosion, what would be the conditions for passing a school-support bill? What set of circumstances is required for such legislation to be enacted in a statesmanlike way *before* a breakdown occurs of so disastrous a scope that senators and representatives are driven to do in hot haste what they might have done gradually and in judicious spirit? From all that has gone before, it can be said that the spontaneous arrangement of circumstances into the ideal pattern is possible—but only in the same way that it is possible for pigments thrown at a canvas to shape themselves into the "Last Supper." That is, it may happen, but it is not a good bet, and to have to count on it for the success of legislation approaches the preposterous.

To sketch out this perfect pattern, the President, to begin with, would have to be more than merely in favor of Federal aid to education—practically everyone is for it in one degree or another, even if it is only to help the schools pay off old bond issues or to give the states a cut of the Federal cigarette taxes paid out by their respective smokers. Going far beyond such minimal notions, the President would have to be for it in a broad and comprehensive way, and feverishly enough to give it a top priority in his program. A bill that ranks downward of fourth on the President's list is assumed to be something he is willing to use for trading purposes with Congress when the going gets hard. It is not "must" legislation, as high priority bills were bluntly designated in the days of the New Deal, but merely one of the counters the executive is prepared to yield in return for passage of those measures he considers truly vital to the success of his administration.

In our dream arrangement the President's party naturally is in control of Congress. If it is the Republicans, a bare majority will do; there will be enough Democrats favorably disposed to such legislation who will help put the measure across. In fact, the smaller the Republican majority, the fewer conservatives it will include, to the natural advantage of such bills as this. In the case of the Democrats, the reverse is true. They need as large a majority as possible, to offset not only the conservative Republican opposition but that of the Southern conservatives in their own ranks.

Given this overall partisan majority, which we have seen is often more nominal than real, it remains to have those who control each center of chopped-up Congressional power committed to the bill, or amenable to their party's expressed will, or at the very least neutralized. The roster includes, in the House, the Speaker, the Majority Leader, the chairman of the Committee on Education and Labor, and the chairman of the Committee on Rules; in the Senate, the Majority Leader, the chairman of the Committee on Labor and Public Welfare, and informally but no less advisedly, an influential leader or two of the Southern bloc, of the caliber, say, of Senator Russell of Georgia.

With all these bases touched, all these crucial spots covered, any bill is almost as good as passed. But if it is rare for such conditions to prevail even for routine bills, it is downright fatuous to expect them for Federal aid to the schools, which is very far from routine. It involves, or at least appears to involve, a major social change, and precisely because it does, the dream pattern is rendered even dreamier than it otherwise would be. Far from eliciting unanimity in the hierarchy of the ruling party, such measures invite conflicting groups and interests to make every use of the roadblocks so conveniently provided by Congressional machinery, to exploit to the full the individual differences of those who operate the levers at the various points of power. It may be inevitable for a controversial measure to provoke division, even within the parties, but only a machine magnificently geared to negation can assure that division of being fatal to the measure's chances, even in modified form. The reconciling of views, the consensus that should be the aim of a legislative body, is sacrificed to the arbitrary power of veto at any of a dozen points along the legislative way.

Of all such ground-breaking measures, the school bills in particular touch sensitive spots on the body politic, a contact that electronically sets off the full nay-saying equipment of the Capitol. The spots in this case are the national tradition that education is exclusively a state and a local responsibility, potential cost, suspicion that Federal aid will be used as a prod to speed up desegregation of Southern schools, and, by far the most sensitive, the two complementary fears: that the Catholic parochial schools will be dealt a mortal blow if they are excluded from a Federal aid program and that, if they are not excluded, Jefferson's wall of separation between church and state will crumble away forthwith.

None of these sensitivities may be as acute in the country itself as they are thought to be in Congress, since members do from time to time mistake the winds on Capitol Hill for the voice of the people; but under the intense barrage of letters and telegrams, they have been warranted in taking the clash of opinion seriously. Another matter, however, is whether they are also warranted in evading the controversy altogether on the ground, commonly advanced, that "You are wrong whatever you do on a bill of this kind." Still less, perhaps, are they warranted, from any civic point of view, in privately encouraging the obstructionist who takes them off the spot. Following the 1961 debacle, *Time* reported a Southern mem-

ber's observation that "when Delaney cast his vote, you could
hear the sigh of relief all over the Capitol." And the reporter
went on to note that hours later, in the Speaker's lobby, Congressmen were still to be seen shaking the hand of the man
who, by bottling up all the aid bills in the Rules Committee,
had spared them the embarrassment of a touchy decision.

In speculating on the future of school legislation, it is well
to take into account, however, that sore spots in public opinion
have a way of becoming desensitized. In any case they are
not equally tender and need not be treated so. In particular
it is hard any longer to regard as a serious concern the first
of the super-sensitivities mentioned, that is, the danger of Federal interference with the schools. For years, as we have seen,
Washington has been at least peripherally involved in the fi-
nancing of education—on the lower levels by way of impacted-
areas legislation and the National Defense Education Act; on
higher levels by way of laws ranging from the Morill Land-
Grant College Act, signed by Abraham Lincoln, down to the
GI Bill and the NDEA of our own day. No Federal tentacles
have yet had to to be pried loose from the school system as
a result.

What is more striking, those who habitually raise the cry
of states' rights in Congress have been constant and enthusiastic in voting renewal of all such Federal interference. No
sooner was the proposed School Assistance Act of 1961 en-
tombed, still alive and kicking, in the Rules Committee, than
the two members of that agency most emphatic about the
dangers of Federal aid voted to extend the impacted-areas
bill. Judge Smith's district received roughly a half-million
dollars in this type of assistance and Colmer's nearly twice
that amount. Senator Goldwater, whose abhorrence of Federal controls is as vocal as that of any man in Washington, proposed amendments to the 1961 bill, though he opposed the
bill itself, which would have required more such control than

anyone had yet proposed. Not only would he have told the
states exactly how they were to spend such funds as they
got from Washington; he would have specified precisely the
academic courses required to make a high school student eli-
gible for his proposed Federal college scholarships—so much
English, so much mathematics, the translation of an original
theme into a foreign language, and so on, all in the interest
of stimulating the student "to get back to the learning of the
three R's." No proponent of Federal aid had ever dared to
suggest intrusion of the national government into this sacred
area of curriculum, for fear of being blown through the sky-
light along with his proposal. But Goldwater drew only the
mild jibe from Senator Morse that "the Senator from Arizona
favors the enactment of a bill which will provide a certain
measure of Federal control, but which will provide very little Federal aid to education."

No doubt there are still some who will vote against any
legislative attempt to pump Federal funds into the nation's
schools solely out of fear that the government might take
them over, but the indications are that they will be only a
remnant of what has for years been a minority in any case.
Given the penetration of Federal aid already suffered and en-
joyed without the socialization of arithmetic, and given the
fact that every serious bill on the subject has contained
guarantees against Federal encroachment on the content of
education, it is difficult to view this issue as anything but a
scarecrow that continues in use long after the crows have
stopped taking fright.

The economy bloc we have always with us, and its usefulness as a check will not be questioned here. Its arguments
with regard to school bills differ in no noticeable way from
the arguments it has made against all social legislation since
the founding of the Republic: A large outlay will shamefully
swell the national debt and bring down on us the curse of

taxpayers yet unborn; and an extremely modest proposal is only the beginning, the ominous intrusion of the camel's foot, or nose, under the tent. (It is hard to imagine, incidentally, what speech makers in Congress would do without this ancient vision of desert tents and camels' anatomies.) But thrift itself, as opposed to thrift as a pretext, has yet to prevail over a great national need, and in the case of schools it is likely to fade before the rising wail of home owners from Long Island Sound to Puget Sound as they try vainly to balance household budget against school budget.

The segregation issue is in a different category altogether. On several occasions, as we have seen, the Powell-type amendment was enough to wreck major legislation to aid the schools, and on others it would surely have done so in the filibustering Senate, had it got that far. Yet the evidence is strong that in this area of legislation the question of segregation, like Federal control, is more a weapon than an issue.

The difficulty is that, as a weapon, it is not as obsolescent as the bogey of Federal control. True, the aid bill of 1960 was passed by the House, Powell amendment and all, but the rider remained a factor in the refusal of the Rules Committee to send the measure to conference—and if the measure had gone to conference with the amendment intact, it is certain that it would never have emerged.

A much more hopeful augury was Mr. Powell's decision in 1961 to refrain from insisting on this hardy perennial, and in fact to oppose it if it were offered by anyone else. Such was his tactical position, as chairman of the House Committee on Education and Labor and in effect as spokesman for the Negro electorate, that attempts by others to inject the question of segregated schools were readily turned back. But it must be admitted that this highly personal approach to a funda-

mental question is limited. Mr. Powell is not a permanent
fixture on Capitol Hill, and the positions he has taken are
even less durable than his tenure. Indeed, two years after the
brave 1961 show he was back at the old stand with the announcement that antidiscrimination amendments on all social
legislation were again in order because the Kennedy Administration was showing signs of "slowing up" on the matter of
civil rights. The problem, in short, cannot be solved on the
basis of satisfying a mercurial individual, any more than the
problems posed by the Rules Committee could be solved by
getting rid of Mr. Colmer—or by adding three new members,
for that matter.

Obviously the difficulty on this score will diminish as the
number of still segregated school districts decreases. It is now
ten years since the Supreme Court's historic edict, and unless
one is ready to write off the Federal system as a mirage,
these segregated districts *will* decrease, since even "with all
deliberate speed" implies a limit beyond which the most indulgent Federal court can no longer allow for the languidness
of the Old South. But short of this long view and expectation,
there is a simple condition, so far as the discrimination issue
goes, for the legislative success of Federal aid. It is simply a
bipartisan understanding among its supporters from the urban
areas of the North, encouraged by the growing need of their
constituents, to vote down all Powell-type amendments to
school bills, regardless of pressures from the district or from
outraged lobbies. This is no more than to say that the lines are
to be kept clear between broad social legislation, needed by
all, and civil-rights legislation, no less essential but a different matter entirely. It would be obligatory on these same Congressmen, not to say politically advisable, to be equally insistent on promoting civil rights, genuinely and in ways that
would yield more concrete results than a school bill pigeonholed or left in shreds on the floor of the House or Senate.

But it is precisely at this point that the machinery of Congress again obtrudes. How are the voters in these urban districts, specifically the Negro voters, to take seriously a Congressman's pledge to promote civil rights *separately* from a school bill when it is a glaring truth that, as presently constituted, the Senate of the United States can no more pass a thorough-going civil rights bill than it can perform *Swan Lake* on the steps of the Capitol?

Any attempt to answer this question must be put off to the end of this work, after we have had a final look at the greatest of all the immediate complexities, the seemingly insoluble problem of the parochial schools.

William V. Shannon, a far more perceptive columnist than most, observed in 1962 that until the fiasco of the preceding year the question of Federal aid to the schools had at least been "a subject of angry controversy and very much alive." But it was so no longer. "In this year's session, the quiet of the tomb settled over the subject. Among politicians of all points of view a consensus has been reached that the religious and philosophical antagonisms engendered by school questions are so bitter that a solution through normal political methods is no longer possible."

Such a consensus would have been a grave indictment of the entire American political system if it had been less heavily charged with the gloom of the moment. Even so, it was a serious reflection on the ability of Congress to perform its function; indirectly, an admission that it could not surmount the obstruction of its own agencies. For there is no reason to suppose that without the trickery of the Rules Committee an agreement would not have been reached in 1961.

In the first place there were not enough Roman Catholics in Congress to have blocked the public school aid bill even if they had been bitterly and unanimously agreed on such a policy. As we know, they were not in agreement at all; indeed, far from being united on the subject, some of their number were to be found at every position in the debate, including those who, like Thompson, led the fight for the very bill denounced by the bishops. Delaney was able to wreck the legislation, not because of a Catholic-Protestant division in Congress or anything resembling it, but simply because he was at one of the numerous control points for arbitrarily snuffing out personally obnoxious bills. It was just that simple.

What is not generally appreciated in this connection is that if a compromise satisfactory to the Delaneys of the House *had* got as far as the Rules Committee, at least three moderate Southerners who were all for a public school aid bill would have joined the usual coalition to kill it. Again, the position taken by these members would not have been open to question, but only the fact that they could so readily impose that position on the entire House. Why try for a consensus when it is so easy not merely to dodge an issue but to have it dodged for you?

Is it genuinely impossible, then, for an understanding to be reached on this subject, an arrangement that would satisfy those who rightfully want to keep state and church from an entanglement that has historically proved harmful to both and at the same time do justice to an unquestionably important part of the country's educational system? It is of course impossible if implacable positions are to be assumed: on the one side that private and parochial schools must receive exactly the same treatment, with taxpayers' money, as the public schools; and on the other, that in no circumstances must they receive public assistance, however undeniably they operate in an area fraught with the public interest.

Where such implacability has in the past been suspended, usually for some highly practical reason, it has been found possible to arrive at an accommodation. The "separation" wall did not crumble when its guardians cheerfully accepted the Veterans' Readjustment Act of 1952, under which ex-soldiers were awarded Federal funds to pay their tuition for any course of their choice, except dancing and bartending, at any school of their choice, whether it was Southern Methodist, Holy Cross, or Hebrew Union. (Would it crumble, then, if parents received a stipend or a tax rebate to pay a child's tuition at Cardinal Hayes High School or the Fieldston School of the Ethical Culture Society?) Neither have these same guardians of the First Amendment—and I share their basic concern— had cause to regret legislation that exempted church-connected schools from taxation and contributed to the lunches of parochial school children, or Supreme Court decisions that approved the expenditure of state funds for their transportation and even for their nonreligious textbooks.

Protest was even less noticeable when the National Defense Education Act of 1958 authorized loans to church and private schools for equipment to improve the teaching of science, languages, and mathematics. The feeling was that the country needed men of science, whether they were inducted into its mysteries in schools provided by the state or the parish. It seems only logical to wonder why loans for buying such equipment are inoffensive, while loans to make possible its use in classrooms of under eighty children should be an unthinkable assault on the wall between church and state.

On the other side, it is pertinent to point out that by no means have all Catholic Church dignitaries, much less all Catholic laymen, taken the uncompromising approach of Cardinal Spellman. Judging by the polls of their districts, reported by such Catholic Representatives as Thompson of New Jersey, Santangelo of New York, and Conte of Massachusetts, a great number of Church adherents, perhaps a majority, are not merely conciliatory but ready to support a bill for helping the public schools first, satisfied merely to hope that in time some way will be found to give assistance to the parochial schools as well.

For this attitude probably no better spokesman can be cited than Cardinal Cushing of Boston, whose commentary on the subject appeared in *The Pilot*, the official organ of his diocese, in October of 1961:

> I feel that as long as the majority of the American people are against such use of taxes, Catholics should try to prove their right to such assistance but neither force such legislation through at the expense of national disunity or use their political influence in Congress to block other legislation of benefit to education because they do not get their own way.

Drowning out this reasonableness, unhappily, is the long record of strident skirmishing, featuring on the one side the 1961 statement of the bishops, which sounded so unfortunately like an ultimatum, and on the other the immovability of those who would rather see no bill at all than one that in any way violates what they are surpassingly certain was the intent of the Founding Fathers.

If the Constitution were as crystal clear about the illegality of Federal funds finding their way to parochial schools as opponents of such aid insist it is—even President Kennedy said "there isn't any room for debate on that subject"—it would be strange indeed for legal scholars to be at any variance at all. Yet for every jurist who takes one side of the debate, one can be found to take the other—and with no appreciable difference in quality. "If I were President," said Arthur Sutherland of Harvard, by way of comment on the Kennedy pronouncement, "I could think of no clear constitutional reason to veto a bill aiding church and private schools." Still more impressive was the long analysis furnished to Senator Morse in the 1961 debate by Mark DeW. Howe, professor of law at the same institution. Philosophically opposed to such a Federal expenditure as he is, Professor Howe nevertheless felt this way as to the law:

> The fact, however, is that these questions of constitutionality—like almost all others—seem to me ultimately to be questions of degree. And when I consider those questions I am satisfied that a valid line may be drawn between governmental support of activities that are predominantly of civil concern and those which are predominantly of religious significance.

Nor have the Justices of the Supreme Court been exactly unequivocal in the matter, as opinions in the *Everson* and *Zorach* cases attest. Justice Douglas in particular gave the First Amendment something of a Delphic quality in his famous pronouncement in the *Zorach* decision: "The First Amendment, however, does not say that in every and all respects there shall be a separation of church and state."

Ideally, Congress would first approach aid to the private schools not as a constitutional question but as a matter of public policy. Should it refuse to use Federal funds to encourage the further fragmenting of the nation's schools? Or should it be concerned above all with the need to elevate the entire educational system as it stands, including the 12 to 13 percent of it that is church-connected? If the decision favored the former course, the verdict would at least be a firm expression of Congressional sentiment, and Church officials could plan accordingly. It is no secret that a number of highly placed Catholic educational authorities, including Father Hesburgh, president of the University of Notre Dame, feel that the parochial system is undergoing a crisis and that if it is not surmounted either the elementary or secondary grades should be dropped, and their pupils transferred to public schools. If, on the other hand, Congress favored some form of help to the parochial schools as part of a general aid program, *then* the question could be faced as to how they could be helped without circumventing the spirit or the letter of the Constitution.

Given this objective, there is little doubt that Congressional ingenuity would be equal to the task. At least three broad approaches have already been staked out, none of which would appear to be drastic departures from precedent. It has already been suggested that long-term loans to private schools for construction of classrooms would scarcely be a legal innovation when those schools are already getting Federal funds for equipment. What is more, there is reason to doubt that the Supreme Court would find a constitutional distinction between loans for the teaching of mathematics, science, and languages for the sake of national defense, and those for reading, writing, and history for the sake of the national welfare. Certainly most laymen would be baffled if the Treasury were allowed to finance the teaching of Goethe in German but not the teaching of Shakespeare in English.

The two other approaches are equally derived from precedent. One would be to appropriate a fixed amount for each pupil, the money going to the state in the event the child attended a public school and, if not, to the parent for tuition at a private school. In effect this would be no more than a downward extension of the GI Bill to the elementary and secondary school level. And the remaining line of attack would be through the tax laws. Here the legal question might well turn on the point of how a deduction for contributing tuition to a church-connected school would be held to breach the wall between church and state when an outright contribution to the church itself is a standard deduction taken by probably 90 percent of the nation's taxpayers.

What should logically hasten the day of compromise in one direction or another is the steady shift in opinion away from the all-out opposition that was once an ideological hallmark of liberalism, as well, ironically, as of bigotry. It was hardly to be foreseen even a decade ago that a bill for loans to parochial schools would be promoted in the Senate, and ardently so, by such recognized members of the liberal fraternity as Wayne Morse and Joseph S. Clark; or that James Reston would use his column in the *New York Times* to chide a Catholic President for failing to see that "The claims of the Catholic Church cannot be lightly brushed aside," that the country "surely needs Catholic brains as well as Baptist or Presbyterian brains." Neither could it be guessed that Walter Lippmann would urge, on behalf of the 5 million children in the parochial schools, that "anything that can be done to help them which does not violate the constitutional principle of separation of Church and State should be done." Or that Dr. Robert M. Hutchins, minimizing the wall of separation, would put the question, "If the Constitution does not require us to leave one-eighth of our children out of a national program of education, why should we do so?" Above all, the swing in public sentiment is a fresh and surprising fact. Of those polled by Dr. Gallup on the subject in 1961, 57 percent favored Federal aid to public schools only, with only 36 percent willing to let Catholic and private schools in on the largesse. The same question put in 1963 elicited a 49 percent decision in favor of including the latter, with only 44 percent for limiting aid to public schools only. What is more, by far the greatest shift took place among the Protestants questioned.

The problem, in short, is not really one of finding a legal formula or of reconciling a bitterly torn population. It is only one of Congressional willingness to make a politically touchy decision and the ability to act on that willingness—in view of the roadblocks that it has itself set up to evade decision and prevent action. The offense in 1961 was not Delaney's—he was entitled to his position and expected to play the game according to the rules. The offense was that Congress provided him with the power to prevent debate, to cut off arbitrarily the process of building a consensus, that very function for which a representative body exists. The question that transcends the fate of school bills and all other legislation is simple enough: Is the country entitled, in matters of the highest importance, to have "the greatest deliberative body in the world" deliberate?

10

First Aid for Congress

From this story of legislative frustration, it is plain that sponsors of Federal aid to the schools have again and again been bilked of their prize solely by the mechanical arrangements of the national legislature. That is to say, they have been beaten not because a majority of the Congress decided, after reasonable thought, that the scheme was contrary to the public good, or for any other such high-sounding reason, but simply because a minority used the arrangements in question to have its own way. As we have seen, a standing committee of the House regularly buried the legislation in the 1940s, sometimes by a single vote; riders and tricky maneuvers killed it on the floor throughout the following decade; and since then it has twice been done to death by that peculiar institution, the Committee on Rules.

Since there is nothing constitutionally prescribed, much less sacred, in the procedures of Congress, the remedies would seem, superficially, to be ready to hand. A deficiency here, a bottleneck there, a disproportion of power somewhere else— surely these should present no technical difficulty to 535 men and women who in the course of duty undertake to adjust the national economy, analyze Pentagon policy, fathom Khrushchev's mind, and serve as Washington's Board of Aldermen.

In fact, the remedies, most of them automatically suggested by the very ills they are intended to cure, have been advanced repeatedly and discussed exhaustively. They are the subject of dozens of books, scores of doctoral theses, and thousands of newspaper editorials, not to mention occasional speeches by mavericks in Congress and even more occasional inquiries by special committees, which it appoints to consider some of the more tepid approaches to reform. The pros and cons of all these proposals can be left to the experts, in Congress and out, the object here being merely to indicate that there is no dearth of prescriptions but only a general reluctance to take medicine.

For the waywardness of arbitrary committee chairmen, the simplest thought is to require fewer signatures on a discharge petition or to make it possible after a fixed time—sufficient, say, to consider the theory of relativity—for a bare majority of the chamber to vote a bill out of limbo. A more basic change is to break the grip of chairmen on their committees by abolishing, or at least weakening, the seniority system, which not only brings the inept to the fore as often as not, but preserves for them a power they never earned. Some have suggested that committee chairmen be picked instead by secret ballot of their colleagues; some, that they be appointed by their party's Congressional caucus, with party loyalty at least one of the criteria in the choice. Still others have suggested that seniority be modified by a rotating system under which a chairman would go to the bottom of the list after a fixed number of terms and work his way up again, thus utilizing experience all along the line without risking the arrogance that goes with certainty of power.

On the two other major fronts, the tyranny of Rules in the House and the tyranny of talk in the Senate, the difficulty, as it is with seniority, is far less a matter of way than of will. Even a restoration of the 21-day rule, touched on in Chapter VII, would pare the claws of the Committee on Rules, which could be further subjected to the changes just suggested for other committees—modified seniority and all. And as the jealous author and guardian of its own procedures, the Senate *could*, so far as the mechanics go, at any time adopt rules to limit its garrulousness and to forbid members to talk about soup greens when the subject under debate is the right to vote, or vice versa.

It must be perfectly obvious, then, that the question of *how* Congress can reform its procedures is less to the point than the question of why it does not do so. For while it is true that the national legislature has always been a shining target for American folk humor—even before Artemus Ward wrote, "Congress, you won't do. Go home, ye mizzerable devils, go home!"—criticisms of its ways have rarely been as severe as they are now and never as deadly serious. It is hard to pick up a newspaper, especially late in a Congressional session, that does not contain some sad or indignant reflection on what the Washington *Post* describes as the "miasma of stagnation" on Capitol Hill. A cross section of the country's political scientists, polled by Senator Case of New Jersey, is of the all but unanimous opinion that, compared with the Executive and Judiciary, Congress is rapidly losing status in the public mind as an effective branch of government. Walter Lippmann, pondering the refusal of Congress for more than a year even to debate the President's fiscal program, finds "reason to wonder whether the Congressional system as it now operates is not a grave danger to the Republic." And from the Capitol itself that sentiment is echoed by Senator Clark: "It is the third

branch of government, the legislative, where things have gone
awry. Whether we look at City Council, the State Legislatures, or the Congress of the United States, we react to what
we see with scarcely concealed contempt. This is the area
where democratic government tends to break down."

The question of why Congress fails to make those procedural adjustments that would at the very least restore its prestige brings us to the heart of the matter, for it involves that
ultimate aspect of republican government, the subtle relationship between the representative and the represented. More
particularly it involves the contract between them which is
constantly up for renewal.

It is safe to assume that extremely few persons go into the
arena of Congressional politics with the desire to serve only a
single term. With such a limitation, especially in the House, a
man's service would be disruptive to his career, expensive, and,
in view of the opportunities for a newcomer, entirely futile.
Neither, of course, can the new member cavalierly court the
possibility of repudiation by the voters the next time around;
his own ego might be impervious to the damage, but his party
would not. His hope and expectation, then, lie in extended
service. And as his terms pile up and his prestige grows, his
private career recedes into the distance and Congress becomes
a settled way of life. Washington tends to spoil its legislators
for the provincial life, and even after defeat, the saying goes,
"They don't go back to Pocatello." But Pocatello does decide
how long they stay on Capitol Hill, and they forget that only
at their peril.

Except in the rarest cases, therefore, the victorious Representative carries with him to Washington a lively preoccupa-
tion with the politics, the distribution of power, and the
sentiment of his district. No matter how deeply the thought of
re-election may be buried, it colors his outlook and determines
his activity: to a very great extent that outlook will be local

and the emphasis of his activity will be on personal service. The effects are far-reaching, having much to do, as we shall see, with the preservation of Congressional machinery in its least attractive aspects.

The spirit of localism in Congress finds its natural expression in the recognized practice of "voting the district." This is the course followed by a Representative who may act on his convictions in matters that are of little or no interest back home, but who will otherwise subordinate those convictions to the views prevailing in his district, or in the case of a Senator, his state. In doing so, he may flout his party, his President, and his conscience, but he will be readily indulged by his colleagues, because "voting the district" is accepted as a valid excuse for all defections. As Speaker of the House, Joseph W. Martin not only defended the practice but advised it. "Unless it was absolutely necessary I never asked a man to side with me if his vote would hurt him in his district," he wrote. "In fact I often counseled members against taking positions on legislation that could cost them the next election."

No doubt this is a far cry from Edmund Burke's famous rebuke to the voters of Bristol: "Your representative owes you, not his industry only, but his judgment; and he betrays instead of serving you if he sacrifices it to your opinion." But in Congress it is the first law of nature. Those who have survived the years to become committee chairmen and powers on the Hill are those who have served local or state interests devotedly, believing perhaps that what is best for Yuma, Arizona, or Birmingham or New York, is *ipso facto* best for the country, but believing it or not, voting that way and thereby rising to the seats of the mighty. D. W. Brogan, that canny observer of American political mores, caught the spirit nicely:

> But an American Congressman who, for the best of reasons, offends local pressure groups, or by not talking for Buncombe, wastes his time on mere national issues of the first order, may

be out—and out forever. The history of Congress is full of martyrs to the general welfare, but any given Congress is full of men who have had more sense than to prefer the general welfare to the local interest.

A corollary to "voting the district" is the personal service rendered by the Congressman to his constituents, from arranging for them to meet a cabinet officer to persuading the cherry blossoms to bloom on schedule for their benefit. There is not a word in the Constitution to suggest that his functions include such duties, but he will habitually decline to do them only at the grave peril of being voted out at the next election. To some extent this has been true for more than a century, but the proficiencies of modern communications have combined to increase the pressure, until today, as we have seen, more than half of a Congressman's time goes to matters having nothing whatever to do with the public business. Out of his long experience in both House and Senate, James F. Byrnes once observed that "The people of a congressional district have come to look upon a Congressman, not as their Representative in Congress, but as their representative in Washington."

To satisfy the often narrow and particular desires of the district and the even narrower and more particular desires of individual constituents, a member of Congress needs an organization, and that is the heart of the problem. He needs an Establishment, if you will, to guarantee that in return for his regularity and support it will see that his private bills go through, that his personal requests are honored, and that he gets his full share of those projects which at their best are good and necessary public works and at their worst are what is known as "pork," a form of political nourishment of questionable public benefit. As he returns to office term after term, in consequence of such services, he himself piles up the seniority which makes it easier for him not only to get the favors he needs, but to be, in turn, a dispenser of favor, a trader, and a power in his own right. In the smooth operating of the system the more seniority he acquires, the greater his bargaining strength, and consequently the greater his continued appeal to his constituents. A district must have a compelling reason indeed to turn out of office a veteran Congressman who has served it well in this material and parochial way, no matter how unorthodox his views may be on such abstruse matters as the Common Market, in favor of a newcomer who can't even be counted on to deliver a new Federal office building.

Inevitably, even innocently, the swapping of favors known as logrolling passes back and forth across the line that separates private and parochial matters from public policy. A member from Rhode Island, for example, is totally indifferent as to whether a peanut research laboratory is located in Georgia or Alabama; but a Representative from one of those states whose district wants the project badly is in a different case, and he is ready to talk trade. If he can get a New Englander's vote in committee, he will in turn go along with him for a boost in the tariff on watches, a cut in foreign-aid appropriations, or even a resolution about outer space.

The great convenience, even the necessity, of a system for assuring the smooth functioning of service to the district accounts in good part for the tenacity with which Congressmen cling to things as they are. Without sources of power there is no dispensing of favor, without favor there is no service, and without service there may be no re-election. The last overhauling of its ways that Congress undertook, in 1946, was authorized only after its sponsors solemnly agreed that no effort would be made to alter the standing rules of legislative procedure. And when the Senate Rules Committee in 1963 approved another such self-appraisal, the resolution carefully stipulated that the special committee set up for the purpose would not consider "rules, parliamentary procedures, practices, or precedents." Which, as the columnist Marquis Childs pointed out, was "like a police chief telling a precinct captain to investigate a series of robberies in his district but not to inquire into the means that were used."

Accordingly, if there is any hope of making Congress primarily the nationally deliberative body that it might be and only secondarily the assembly of sectional and provincial representatives that to some extent it must be, the hope lies, I think, in the direction of making its members somewhat freer than they are of local whim and sentiment. To probe the relationship between the leaders of a republic and the led would require another, and no doubt more philosophic, work, but suggestions for the liberation of Congressmen in this respect are probably in order even in passing.

To free an elected official from slavish service to his constituents, as distinct from the mutually respectful ties that ought to exist, two elementary courses are open: lengthen his term of office and limit the number of terms. The first gives him time to learn the ropes and develop a course of action free from the preposterous pressure of having to start campaigning again the day after he takes the oath. The limitation on terms, by eliminating Congress as a way of life and ultimately ridding the member's mind of any thought of re-election, rids it likewise of the fears and the demagoguery that constant electioneering has been known to inspire. A four-year term for Representatives, with a three-term limit, a scheme proposed by Representative Thomas B. Curtis of Missouri and endorsed by President Eisenhower, would require a Constitutional amendment and therefore *could* originate outside of Congress, an advantage in view of the established reluctance of that body to take any initiative concerning its own possible improvement. Far from incidentally, the arrangement would also solve the problem of protracted tenure for committee chairmen, thus eliminating by far the worst aspect of seniority. If after a suitable interlude a retired Representative wished to re-enter the lists, he would be free to do so, his experience intact but his seniority to be acquired all over again.

A greater and more daring encouragement to a nationally minded Congress would be a lifting of the ban against the candidacy of "outsiders." Under the Constitution a Representative or Senator must be an inhabitant of the state in which he is chosen. Technically this is not much of a barrier, since he can re-establish residence quickly enough. But tradition, which is much stricter, requires as a rule not only a fairly long identity with the state but, in the case of Representatives, with the district as well. The most obvious result is that a Louisiana or Manhattan Republican with Congressional aspirations, no matter how gifted he may be, is out of the running unless he is willing, able and smart enough, early in his career, to pull up stakes and settle, say, in Indiana or Long Island instead. Much more important, a Congressman who in time transcends the prejudices of his district is politically finished; he cannot, except after many years, expect to pick up his legislative career in a district more congenial to his views. Such restrictions do not exist in England or even in neighboring Canada. In either case a politician can shop around for a riding and, being less rigidly bound to one little corner of the earth, is the freer to weigh questions of national and international import.

No doubt a scheme for free-floating Congressmen, on the Anglo-Canadian model, would run into prejudices left over from the earliest days of the Republic, when a Georgian and a Pennsylvanian were not certain that they wanted to be in the same country, much less in the same assembly. They had real sectional differences, often of an acute social and economic sort, to account for their feelings. But there would seem to be a far greater clash of interests today between voters within a state, say a New Yorker from Westchester County and one from 125th Street in Manhattan, than between members of the same social group in different states. A New York Congressman who represents millionaire and slum dweller alike should have little trouble adapting himself to the needs of voters in Boston, St. Louis, or Los Angeles.

Naturally logic would set its own limits. Even without a legal ban, it is improbable that a Herbert Lehman would be nominated in the hills of Tennessee or a Calvin Coolidge in Brooklyn. But with the increasing standardization of the country, sectionalism is not the predominant political factor it once was. Not many good things can be said for such standardization perhaps, but one might well be that it would allow Congressmen greater mobility—both geographically and ideologically.

Could a "foreigner" really know the general needs of his newly adopted district? Obviously he would learn them quickly enough or find it prudent to move on. What he might *not* be relied on to know or to master in short order are the particular services that particular individuals, businesses, and organizations would expect of him in his capacity as errand-boy or Washington agent, a role that unhappily would consume more of his time and make more of an impression, good or bad, than his performance as a legislator. It is at this point that a companion, and less arguable, proposal for lifting the sights of Congressmen might be considered.

If Representatives and Senators could be relieved of the burden of private bills and personal services, the time and energy they could devote to the public business would be doubled and their reliance on the machinery of an Establishment greatly reduced. Under the staggering load of trivia, many members have called out for help, but the only answer has been the increase allowed in the size of their office staffs, which, in view of the increasing pressure of requests has been no answer at all. For adjusting small claims on the government—like the bill introduced in a recent Congress to reimburse a Mississippi farmer $150 for a heifer "which died as a result of consuming part of a weather balloon of the United States"—there is no answer, ultimately, but a quasi-judicial agency, responsible either to Congress or to part of the Executive branch. For both efficiency and justice nothing makes less sense than the continued requirement that each of these myriad claims be treated as a bill, subject to all the agonies of the legislative process and politically obligating its sponsor to those who can speed it through the procedural mill.

As for the errand-boy aspects of Congressional life, at least as time consuming as the handling of private bills, no fresher idea has been advanced, to my knowledge, than the proposal of Representative Henry S. Reuss of Wisconsin, with a nod of acknowledgment to the Swedish Riksdag. The suggestion is to establish here an office somewhat like that of the Swedish *ombudsman*, an official who serves as a citizen's agent, as it were, in all his dealings with officialdom, both civil and military. The American counterpart of the *ombudsman* might well be a major agency, modeled on the Comptroller General's Office, rather than an individual or two, and its function could extend to all manner of services that are now demanded of the hard-pressed legislator. It would see that this complainant's social security account got straightened out, that another's request for an altered draft status was fairly heard, that a third was given the opportunity to make a proper bid for a defense contract, and a fourth got a fair hearing for having his wife's cousin admitted, or perhaps deported, as an exception under the immigration laws. The agency would be a slasher of red tape, an honest intermediary between the bemused citizen and the bewildering bureaucracy. It would replace both the influence peddler and, in this role, the harried Congressman, who again would find himself with more time to legislate and less dependence on the Club for expediting such services to his constituents.

It may be noted that in this conclusion I have touched only lightly on specific procedural changes in those areas that are the common concern of Congressional reformers—seniority, the Rules Committee, unlimited debate, and the like. The entire book, I trust, is an argument for such changes, and I am at this point concerned not with the particular improvements to be made—these can be left to the technical experts on the Hill—but with those larger changes that would free Congressmen to make the others.

Neither have I considered at all those potential and sweeping rearrangements that are the special concern of the political scientists—elimination of the noncompetitive, one-party districts; party responsibility in Congress; and perhaps the realignment of the parties themselves to conform to the broad ideological concepts found in the electorate. As changes that might flow from the political and social development of the country, these can be expounded and discussed but not demanded. They are the hoped-for consequences of historic transformations, possibly to be predicted and even encouraged, but hardly to be prescribed.

The proposals dealt with here are, by contrast, on a modest working level. Yet by freeing the individual Congressman from the demands of a narrow parochialism, by undermining the rule of seniority, by weakening the leverage of committee chairmen and the need for a systematized exchange of favor, they would at the very least create a thaw in which rules could be changed, even the filibuster—in which machinery could be modernized and gross irrelevancies discarded. They would not bring in the millennium, but they could make the Congress of the United States more sensitive to the public need, more deliberate in seeking ways to respond, and more capable, once it reached a consensus, of translating its opinion into law.

I do not believe that the Congresses of our time, man for

man, suffer in the least by comparison with those of the past. In some respects—mastery of complex material and dollar honesty among them—ours are very likely superior in talent to those of the nineteenth century. Critics who complain that the Senate no longer boasts men of the caliber of Clay, Calhoun, and Webster are referred to the similar plaint of Alexis de Tocqueville. When those giants still spoke in the land, the keen French observer commented sadly that "the race of American statesmen has evidently dwindled most remarkably in the course of the last fifty years." That would seem to argue that if we *have* been going downhill, there is at least nothing new about a decline that began in 1789.

There is far more reason to believe, however, that the decline of Congress is not at all in the quality of its membership; it is a decline brought on, in good part, by the swift and complex movement of the modern world and its own failure, for which it is accountable, to adapt itself to change. Congress is slowed down, held back, often rendered impotent, by institutional growths which time and circumstances have allowed to leech on to it. When these serve, like monstrous parasites, to drain away the vitality of the national legislature, they become the concern—or should—not only of technicians, but of all who have a stake in keeping the popular branch of government from slipping to the level of an anachronism.

That should include roughly the entire population; but the truth is, of course, that the matter disturbs the sleep of no more than a handful of Americans. If this work adds a few more to their number, it will have served its purpose. Maybe the others are busy today and will get around to the problem tomorrow, as many Frenchmen no doubt intended to do right up to the day that General DeGaulle took over their maladroit and somewhat moth-eaten parliament.

The author has gratefully dipped into the following wells of information, observation, and wisdom:

The Legislative Struggle, by Bertram Gross
Congress at the Crossroads, by George B. Galloway
History of the House of Representatives, by George B. Galloway
Grammar of American Politics, by Wilfred E. Binkley and Malcolm C. Moos
Member of the House, by Clem Miller
A Bill Becomes a Law, by Daniel M. Berman
Congress Makes a Law, by Stephen K. Bailey
Congressional Government, by Woodrow Wilson
U.S. Senators and Their World, by Donald R. Matthews
The Deadlock of Democracy, by James MacGregor Burns
Forge of Democracy, by Neil MacNeil
A 20th-Century Congress, by Estes Kefauver and Jack Levin
Federal Aid to Education, Special Report published by *Congressional Quarterly*
National Politics and Federal Aid to Education, by Richard F. Fenno, Jr., and Frank J. Munger
"Race, Religion and the Rules Committee" in *The Uses of Power,* edited by Alan F. Westin
My First Fifty Years in Politics, by Joseph Martin
Yankee from the West, by Burton K. Wheeler

221

Index

Adams, John Quincy, 32
Adams, Sherman, 134
Aiken, George D., 77–78, 80
Alger, Bruce, 124, 135
Allen, Leo J., 145–146
Alter, Archbishop Karl J., 181
Amending process, 25–27, 115–117
    pro forma amendments, 102, 118, 188
    tabling an amendment, 117
American Association of School Administrators, 51
American Farm Bureau, 132, 177
American Federation of Teachers, 51, 78–79, 92
American Legion, 51, 132
American Telephone and Telegraph Co., 41
Americans for Democratic Action, 126, 133
Area redevelopment bill, 61, 153–154, 166
Arends, Leslie C., 136
Aspinall, Wayne N., 62
Ayres, William H., 133, 135–136, 139

Bailey, Cleveland, 133, 163, 165–167, 185

Bailey, Stephen K., 38
Barden, Graham, 79–81, 88, 90–96, 122, 127, 159–160, 166, 180
Barkley, Senator Alben, 25, 105
Bills, 1–17
    action by conference committees, 28–29
    amending, 25–26, 27, 114–117
    assignment to committee, 18–19
    "clean," 21
    debate on, 22, 56
    discharge petitions, 23–24
    dropped in hopper, 17
    hearings, 26
    introducing, 17–18
    methods of killing, 24–25, 115–118
    move to reconsider vote after passage, 118
    move to strike out enacting clause, 25, 117, 137–139
    noncontroversial, 103
    number introduced, 19
    obstacles, 16–17
    originating in executive branch, 39–40
    passage, 29
    powers of Rules Committee, 21–23, 31
    (*See also* Rules Committee)

223

Bills, Presidential veto, 30
    printed transcripts, 26
    priority assigned to, 59, 142–144
    private, 17, 24, 212, 216–217
    procedure through Congress, 15–
        31
        House of Representatives, 15–
            26
        Senate, 26–31
    recommitting to committee, 22–
        24, 116–117
    reporting out, 21
    "riders," 26, 115–116
    screening process, 19–20
    signing, 29–30
    sponsors, 18, 28, 102
    tabled by committees, 21
    weak vs. strong, 39
Blatnik, John A., 172, 178
Bolling, Richard, 125, 136, 152, 187
Brademas, John, 166
Bricker amendment, 60
British Parliament, 16, 57
Brogan, D. W., 208–209
Brown, Clarence, 151, 155, 179
Budget, Federal, 32–33
Burke, Edmund, 211
Burns, James MacGregor, 149n
Byrd, Harry F., 54
Byrnes, James F., 212

"Calendar Wednesday," 151, 153–
    154, 166, 188
Cannon, Clarence, 61, 66
Cannon, Speaker Joseph, 26, 31,
    143, 149
Cannonism, 144, 150
Case, Clifford P., 209
Childs, Marquis, 213–214
Christian Century, 49
Church and state, separation of, 49–
    52, 194, 200–203
Civil rights legislation, 23
    delays, 61
    filibusters over, 111, 113
    public accommodation provisions,
        19
    special interest groups, 41
    use of riders, 115–116

Clark, Joseph S., 57, 164, 205
    on Congressional reform, 69–70,
        73, 104–105, 209
Clark, Speaker Champ, 17
Clay, Henry, 32
Clayton Act, 39
Cloture, 27, 113
Colmer, William M., 126, 174–175,
    187–188, 195, 198
Committees, Congressional, 54–66
    assigning bills to, 18–19
    assignments, 69–71
    chairmen, 54, 208
        arbitrary powers of, 58–60, 66
        control over agenda, 58–60
        control over subcommittees,
            60–61, 63
        power to postpone meetings,
            61–66
        relations with President, 66
    criticism of, 57–58
    defection from leadership, 71–72
    geographical composition, 70
    hearings, 64
    need for, 55–57
    party responsibility, 72–73
    powers, 54–66
    reciprocal courtesy, 65, 104
    reorganization of, 82
    reporting a bill out, 21–22
    reports, 56
    seniority, 64–65, 66–68, 209,
        212–213
    Southern control of, 67–68
    standing, 19
    subcommittees, 60–61, 63
Conference committee, 28–29
    refusal to send school bill to, 168–
        171
Congress, 15–31
    committees (see Committees,
        Congressional)
    functions, 15
    legislative powers, 57
        (See also Legislative process)
    legislative reorganization, 82
    procedures, 15–31
        adjustments needed, 207–219
        rivalry between two branches, 28

Congress, status of, 209–210, 218–219
    traditions, 31
    weaknesses, 37
Congressional Record, 16, 32, 99–100, 108, 116
Congressmen, bargaining strength, 213
    new, 17–18
    nonlegislative work, 56
    office staffs, 57*n*, 216
    personal services for constituents, 211, 212, 216–217
    re-election of, 213
    residence requirements, 215–216
    salaries and allotments, 57*n*
    tenure, 214
    voting the district, 211–212
Constituents, 56, 211–212, 216–217
Cooper, John Sherman, 164
Constitution, on Congressional procedures, 31
Coolidge, Calvin, 30, 71
Council of Chief State School Officers, 51
Cox, Eugene, 142, 145
Curtis, Thomas B., 178, 214
Cushing, Richard Cardinal, 202

Daughters of the American Revolution, 51
Dawson, William L., 125
Debate on bills, 22
    extended, 110–111
    (*See also* Floor procedures)
Delaney, James J., 187–188, 195, 200, 205
Democratic Study Group, 172–174
Democrats, Northern, 73, 144–145
    Senate Steering Committee, 69
    Southern, 68, 72, 124, 144
        coalition with Republicans, 167, 179
Dirksen, Senator Everett, 105, 110, 164
Discharge petitions, 23–24, 151–153, 156, 208
Dixiecrats, 72

Douglas, Paul, 57, 65, 70
Douglas, William O., 203

Eastland, James O., 19, 60–63, 67
Eberharter, Rep., 147
Education, state and local responsibility, 191, 194
    (*See also* Federal Aid to education)
80th Congress, 82–90
81st Congress, 154
82nd Congress, 154
83rd Congress, 106, 120
84th Congress, 119, 120
85th Congress, 131
86th Congress, 160, 167, 173
87th Congress, 28, 55, 58, 62, 101, 103, 148, 173
88th Congress, 54–55, 70, 113, 180–189
Eisenhower, Dwight D., 214
    school-aid proposals, 121, 125, 130–135, 138–139, 159, 163–165, 168, 170
Ellender, Allen J., 43, 76, 80
Elliott, Carl, 161, 180
Enacting clause, 25, 117
    used to kill school-aid bill, 137–139
"Establishment, The," 57, 69, 70, 73, 105
Everson and *Zorach* cases, 203
Executive branch, legislative proposals originating in, 39–40, 57
Executive messages, 39

Fabius the Delayer, 98
Federal aid to education, 32–52, 74–97
    achieving consensus, 42, 194, 205–206
    amount expended, 36–191
    behind-the-barn approach, 34–35
    for colleges, 188
    conditions for passing a bill, 192–206
    defeated by coalition of Republicans and Democrats, 167
    80th Congress, 82–90

Federal aid to education, 81st Congress, 90–97
  83rd Congress, 120
  84th Congress, 119, 120
  85th Congress, 131
  88th Congress, 180–189
  enacting clause used to kill bill, 137–139
  equalization principle, 90, 95
  fear of federal interference, 195
  fixed amounts for each child, 204
  floor proceedings, 119–139
  hearings, 76–79, 85–86, 88–89, 92–93, 96, 132
  historical background, 32–34, 74–75
  to impacted areas, 35, 44, 185, 195
  Kelley bill, 121–124, 127, 133, 136
  killed in the Rule Committee, 157–189
  loans for private schools, 182–183, 204–205
  McNamara bill, 163
  Murray-Metcalf bill of 1958, 159–163, 170
  National Defense Education Act, 36
  need for, 75, 190–191
  Negro community and, 44–46
  1956 campaign issue, 130
  1960 campaign issue, 170
  opposition to, 51, 76, 79
  parochial school issue, 77–80, 85, 88, 92–205, 119, 162–164, 181–183, 186, 194, 199–206
  party support, 193
  position of Deep South, 42–44
  Powell amendment, 45–46, 122–130, 133, 135, 167, 186, 197
  Presidential backing needed, 192–193
  professional education groups, 50–51
  public opinion polls, 36–37
  reconciling group conflicts, 42, 194, 205–206
  religious issue, 46–49

Federal aid to education, Roman Catholic Church and, 46–49, 162–164, 181–183
  for school construction, 131, 162, 181
  segregation issue, 43–46, 194, 197–199
  separationists, 49–52, 194, 200, 203
  79th Congress and, 74–82
  Smith's refusal to send to Conference, 168–171
  special interest groups favoring, 41–52
  Spellman-Roosevelt argument, 93–94
  tax deductions, 204
  for teachers' salaries, 84, 86, 90, 162, 164, 168, 180
  Thompson bill, 186–187
  for transportation and textbooks, 90, 94
  Wainwright antisegregation amendment, 133–134
Fenno, Richard F., 83, 119n
Filibusters, 27, 70–71, 110–113, 117, 218
  extended debate differs from, 110–111
Floor proceedings, 56, 119, 139
  amending process, 114–116
  delaying tactics, 98–118
  extended debate, 110–111
  federal aid to education, 119–139
  filibusters, 110–113, 117
  parliamentarian, 105
  roll and quorum calls, 101–102
  rules agreed on for debate, 102–103, 107–110
Folsom, Marion B., 132, 134
Foreign-aid program, 66
Freylinghuysen, P., Jr., 120, 134, 166, 185–186
Friends of the Public Schools of America, 76
Fries, Maj. Gen. Amos A., 76
Fulbright, J. William, 61, 185
Full Employment Act, 38

Gallup, Dr. George, 36, 205
German, George B., 34
Goldwater, Barry, 163, 168, 195–
    196
G.I. Bill, 195
Green, Edith, 161
Gross, Bertram M., 106
Gwinn, Rep., 88–89, 127–129

Halleck, Charles A., 136–138, 167,
    169–170, 173, 176, 178–179
Harlow, Bryce N., 125
Harrison, Senator Pat, 43
Hart, Merwin K., 77
Hartley, Fred, 83–84, 88–89
Hearings on bills, 26, 64
    joint, 87
Henderson, John, 124
Hendrickson, Senator, 108
Hennings, Senator, 61
Herter, Christian A., 147
Hesburgh, Father, 203
Hill, Senator Lester, 43, 75, 80, 84,
    90
Hobby, Oveta Culp, 121, 132
Hochwalt, Msgr. Frederick G., 48,
    77–78, 182, 184, 186
Hoffman, Clare, 124, 156
Hollander, Edward D., 133
Hosmer, Craig, 116
House of Representatives, 15–26
    Agriculture Committee, 70
    Appropriations Committee, 58,
        61, 66, 103, 152
    Armed Services Committee, 66
    Committee of the Whole, 101–
        102, 117, 138
    Committee on the District of Co-
        lumbia, 20, 58
    Committee on Interior and In-
        sular Affairs, 62
    delay-and-conquer tactics, 98–
        118
    Education and Labor Committee,
        82–84, 89–90, 119, 132
    liberal members, 161
    membership, 99
    Rules Committee (see Rules
        Committee)

House of Representatives, rules for
    debate, 102–103, 107–110
    Speaker, 99, 103
    typical session, 99–100
    Ways and Means Committee, 58,
        59, 66, 69
Housing bills, 18
Howe, Mark DeW., 202–203
Humphrey, Hubert, 18n, 185, 189
Hutchins, Dr. Robert M., 158, 205

Illiteracy, 75–76
Impacted areas, school-aid for, 35,
    44, 195.
Inouye, Daniel, 71
Integration, Supreme Court decree,
    43, 45, 121
Investment Bankers Association,
    132
Irwin, Don, 136

Jackson, Andrew, 33
Javits, Jacob K., 164
Jefferson, Thomas, 27–28
Jenner, Senator, 158
Johnson, Lyndon B., 66, 115–116,
    162, 164, 168–169, 173, 177

Kefauver, Senator, 60
Kelly, Augustine, 121–124, 135
Kelley bill, 121–124, 127, 133, 136
Kennedy, John F., 19
    on federal aid to education, 48–
        49, 94, 172–173, 180–181,
        188, 202, 205
    legislative program, 54–55
    tax proposals, 66
Kilgore, Harley, 60
King, Senator, 32
Klein, Herbert G., 169
Knoff, Dr. Gerald E., 50

Labor unions, bills concerning, 18
LaFollette, Senator Robert, 71–72
Langer, Senator, 45, 115
Legislative process, 37–42
    origins of a law, 37–42
    power of organizations, 40

Legislative process, proposals originating in Executive branch, 39–40
role of public, 37
(*See also* Bills)
Lens, Sidney, 64
Lesinski, John, 79–80, 88, 90, 93–96
Life, 36
Lincoln, Abraham, 195
Lindsay, John V., 156
Lippmann, Walter, 191, 205, 209
Lobbies, 40, 50
Lodge, Henry Cabot, the Elder, 114
Longworth, Nicholas, 72
Lutheran Church, 50

McCaskill, James L., 130
McClellan, John 43
McConnell, Rep. Sam, 96–97, 119, 129, 134
McCormack, John, 124, 182–183, 186
McGrath, Earl J., 90
McManus, Fr. William E., 47, 78, 85
McNamara, Patrick V., 158, 162–163
MacNeil, Neil, 179
Madden, Ray, 187
Magnuson, Warren G., 19
Mansfield, Senator Mike, 54, 182, 185
Marsh, Benjamin C., 79, 86
Martin, Speaker Joseph W., 89, 134, 145, 164
Matthews, Donald R., 112
Meany, George, 126
Medical care for the aged, 58
Metcalf, Lee, 136, 149, 158, 161–162, 172
Miller, Clem, 141
Mills, Wilbur, 66
Mitchell, Clarence, 45–46
Morill Land-Grant College Act, 195

Morse, Wayne, 72, 106, 112, 164, 181, 184–185, 196, 202–203, 205
Moynihan, Daniel P., 49
Munger, Frank J., 119n
Murray, James E., 76, 80, 158, 160

National Anti-Saloon League, 40
National Association for the Advancement of Colored People, 44–46, 77
National Association of Manufacturers, 40, 132, 161, 177
National Catholic Welfare Conference, 46–48, 78, 181, 186
National Congress of Parents and Teachers, 51
National Council of the Churches of Christ in America, 50
National Defense Education Act, 36, 48, 157–159, 183, 185–188, 195–201
National Education Association, 50, 75, 78, 121, 125, 132, 163, 170, 188–189
National Grange, 51
Negroes, position on federal aid to education, 44–46
New Deal, 145
New York *Herald Tribune,* 136–137
New York Times, 55, 90, 205
Newsweek, 186
Nixon, Richard, 95, 164, 168–171
Norris, George W., 112–113, 144
Northwest Ordinance, 34
Norton, John K., 76, 85, 88
Norton, Mary, 83

O'Brien, Lawrence, 185
O'Neill, Thomas P., 187
Orwell, George, 17
Oxnam, Bishop G. Bromley, 93

Parochial school issue, 46–50, 77, 80, 85, 88, 91–95, 162–164, 181–183, 186, 194, 199–206
Passman, Otto, 66

Pastore, John O., 110
Peoples Lobby, Inc., 79, 86
Perry, Leslie S., 77, 85
Political power, 73
Populist leaders, 38
Pork barrel projects, 24, 212
Powell, Adam Clayton, 46, 106–107, 180, 187–188, 197–198
Powell amendment, 51, 122–130, 133, 135, 167, 169, 186
Presidency, program, 53–55
  relations with committee chairmen, 66
  relations with Congress, 53–54
  tenure, 53
  veto power, 30
Price, H. Douglas, 181n
Private bills, 17, 24, 212, 216–217
Pro forma motions, 102, 118, 188
Protestants and Others United for Separation of Church and State, 49
Proxmire, William, 70
Public's role in legislative process, 37
Public lands, 34
Public opinion polls, on federal aid to education, 36

Quorum calls, 101

Ramspeck, Rep., 75
Rauh, Joseph L., Jr., 63
Rayburn, Sam, 23, 101, 161, 171–180
Recommitting bills to committee, 116–117
Reconsideration of vote after passage of bill, 118
Reece, Rep., 166–169
Reed, Daniel A., 146
Reed, Thomas B., 143
Reporter, The, 49
Republicans, coalition with Southern Democrats, 167, 179
  control of committees, 68
  Southern, 68, 72
Reston, James, 66, 205

Reuss, Henry S., 217
Ribicoff, Abraham, 183, 185
Riders on bills, 115–116
  attached to bills, 26
Roberts, Owen J., 146
Roll calls, 101–102
Roman Catholic Church, 162–164, 181–183, 186
  on federal aid to education, 46–49, 162–164, 181–183
Rooney, John, 66
Roosevelt, Eleanor, 93–94
Roosevelt, Franklin Delano, 144–145
Roosevelt, James, 129, 161, 172
Roper, Elmo, 36–37
Rules Committee, 21–23, 29n, 31, 140–156
  able to kill bills outright, 147
  arguments against, 151–152
  arguments for, 150–151, 155–156
  attempts to reform, 154–155
  changes in bills forced by, 147
  civil rights bill, 148
  concentration of powers, 22, 31, 142–156
  criticism of, 22–24, 29n, 172, 209
  demand for reform, 172
  Eisenhower Administration, 146
  enlargement of, 176
  fair trade bills, 148
  liberal bloc, 172–173
  meetings, 141–142
  misuse of power, 156
  power to override legislation, 169
  priorities of bills assigned by, 59, 142–144
  proposal for purge, 174
  Roosevelt Administration, 144–145
  "suspension of the rules," 153
  time limit on debate fixed by, 143
  Truman Administration, 145
  21-day rule, 154–155, 173, 209
  tyranny of, 209
Russell, Richard B., 71n, 110

Sabath, Adolph, 142, 151
Segregation issue, 43–46, 194, 197–199
Senate, 26–31
  Armed Services Committee, 71–72
  attendance, 104–105
  Banking and Currency Committee, 58, 61
  bills, 26–31
    scheduling, 21–22, 27
  chamber, 104
  Democratic Steering Committee, 69
  District of Columbia Committee, 103n
  filibusters, 27, 70–71, 110–113, 117, 218
  Judiciary Committee, 61, 63, 65, 67, 115
  Labor and Public Welfare Committee, 90
  Majority Leader, 21–22, 27
  party leaders, 21–22
  power to fix priorities on bills, 21–22
  reciprocal courtesy, 65, 104
  rules for debate, 103–104, 107–110
Seniority of committee members, 64–68, 209, 212–213, 218
Separation of church and state, 49–52, 194, 200–203
Separation of powers, 55
79th Congress, 74–82
Shannon, William V., 199
Sherman Anti-Trust Act, 38–39
Sisk, B. F., 180
Smith, Senator Hoke, 43
Smith, Howard W., 23, 136–137, 166
  Chairman of Rules Committee, 146–150
  power struggle with Rayburn, 174–180
  refusal to send school bill to conference, 168–171
Southern Democrats, 68, 72, 124, 144

Southern Democrats, coalition with Republicans, 167, 179
  control of Congressional committees, 67–68
  position on federal aid to education, 42–44
Space communications satellite program, 41
Speaker of the House, 99, 103
  functions of, 143–144
  powers of, 31
Spellman, Francis Cardinal, 48, 93–95, 186, 201
Sponsors for bills, 18, 28, 102
Standing committees (see Committees, Congressional)
Statehood bills, 146–148
States' rights, 42, 47
States' Rights Democrats, 72–73
Stevenson, Adlai, 72, 130
"Strike the enacting clause," 25, 117, 137–139
Stuart, Justine, 40n
Supreme Court's decree for integration, 43, 45, 121
Sutherland, Arthur, 202

Taft, Robert A., 81–82, 84, 103n, 127
Taft-Hartley Act, 83
Tax proposals, 54–55, 66
Thompson, Frank, 136, 160–161, 165–166, 172, 181–183, 200–201
Thurmond, Strom, 111–112
Time, 194
Trimble, James W., 169
Truman, Harry, 72, 89, 94–95, 125, 145

Udall, Stewart, 136, 138, 161, 166–167, 172, 177
United States Chamber of Commerce, 51, 77, 132

Van Buren, Martin, 33
Veterans' Readjustment Act of 1952, 201

Vinson, Carl, 64–66, 176
Voorhis, Jerry, 70
Voting records, 26

Wainwright, Stuyvesant, 133–134
Walter, Francis, 129
Washington, George, 27–28, 39
Washington home-rule bills, 20, 58
Washington *Post*, 144, 166, 209
Welfare state, 34
Wheeler, Burton K., 59, 60

Wheeler, Wayne B., 40n
Wier, Roy, 122
Wilderness preservation bill, 62
Williams, John J., 106–107
Wilson, Woodrow, 27, 39, 54, 55, 112
Women's   Christian   Temperance
   Union, 40

Young, Stephen M., 105

Zelenko, Rep., 186–187

About the Author

Robert Bendiner's articles have appeared over a period of twenty-five years in *Harper's, The Saturday Evening Post, The New York Times Magazine, Life, Look,* and other periodicals. A former managing editor of *The Nation* and contributing editor of *The Reporter,* Mr. Bendiner was also American correspondent for the *New Statesman.* A recipient of the Benjamin Franklin magazine award for his article "The Engineering of Consent—A Case Study in Public Relations," Mr. Bendiner was awarded a Guggenheim Fellowship in 1962. He is the author of *White House Fever,* published in 1960, and is currently president of the Society of Magazine Writers.